Home Sweet Home

Home Sweet Home

Building Collaborations to Keep Families Together

Yvonne A. Doerre

Lisa Klee Mihaly

CWLA Press • Washington, DC

CWLA Press is an imprint of the Child Welfare League of America, Inc.

CHILD WELFARE LEAGUE OF AMERICA, INC.
440 First Street, NW, Third Floor, Washington, DC 20001-2085
Email: books@cwla.org

CURRENT PRINTING (last digit)
10 9 8 7 6 5 4 3 2 1

Cover and text design by Alexhon Electronic Publishing

Printed in the United States of America
ISBN # 0–87868–653–3

Contents

Acknowledgments

The research and technical assistance that produced the information in this manual were made possible by the generous support of the Annie E. Casey Foundation. The Robert Wood Johnson Foundation funded previous work by CWLA that also contributed to these efforts.

This guide is a testament to all the wonderful collaborative work currently going on in communities across the country for the benefit of vulnerable children and families. It aims to celebrate these practices and to serve as a resource for communities beginning and/or expanding similar programs. CWLA is grateful to all the program directors who contributed information to this document. We especially want to thank all the contact people listed in Appendix A. Their programs are marked with a ❤ symbol in the text, and they are making themselves available for further consultation.

Allan Katz, a health care consultant based in California, has been an active participant in CWLA's housing/child welfare collaboratives. Allan wrote the Primary Health Care section of this manual; his knowledge and insight has added much to our efforts.

The authors, along with everyone involved with the Family Unification Program, owe a huge debt of gratitude to David Liederman, CWLA executive director, and the CWLA Public Policy Department. Without their tireless advocacy for children and families, the Family Unification Program would not exist.

Our sincere thanks to Senator Christopher Bond (R) of Missouri and his legislative staff. Senator Bond has ensured the continued funding of FUP each year since 1992. For his leadership on behalf of vulnerable families, we are very grateful.

CWLA's Family Unification Program Advisory Committee reviewed drafts of this manual and offered invaluable critiques and suggestions. Our thanks to the members of the committee, who are listed in Appendix A.

Our appreciation to Jerry Benoit and Bill Murphy of the Division of Public and Indian Housing, HUD. Their graciousness in working with CWLA while administering the FUP has facilitated the creation of a national network of information and assistance for agencies implementing housing and support programs.

Thanks also to Bob McKay, who leads all CWLA housing activities. This manual benefited from the guidance of Bronwyn Mayden, the expert editing of Mary Liepold, and the assistance of Angela Grigsby. The Children's Defense Fund granted permission to use material developed by Lisa Mihaly during her work with that sister organization. Many thanks to all.

Home Sweet Home is dedicated to families in every community across the country who have suffered unnecessary separation because they lacked adequate housing. We hope that our efforts and those of committed professionals from coast to coast can ease their suffering and help them find the decent, affordable housing they need.

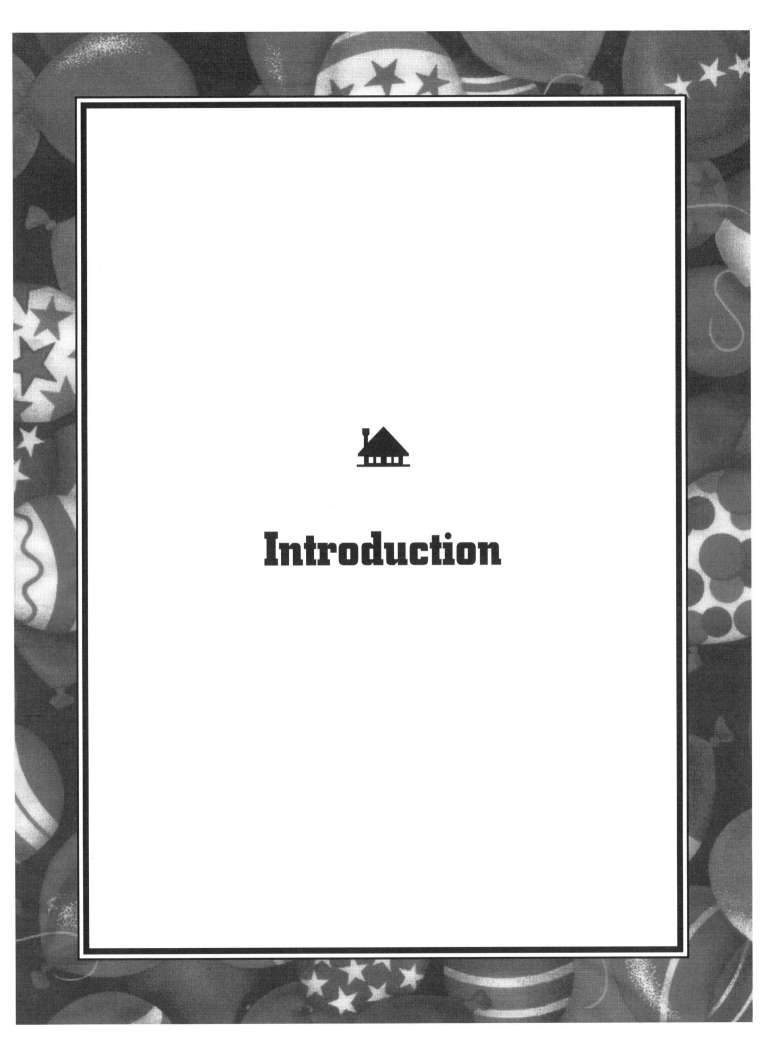

Introduction

Safe, affordable housing is a cornerstone of stable family life. The majority of American families take this resource for granted and could never imagine it being in jeopardy. However, stable housing is becoming beyond the reach of a large and growing minority of families. Families in communities around the country struggle to find and maintain housing that meets their needs. Homelessness or persistent substandard housing place enormous burdens on a family, and often precipitates its breakup.

Increasingly, child welfare workers are seeing children come into out-of-home care due largely to their family's lack of adequate housing. They also see children remain in care because their families lack adequate housing. Together, local child welfare agencies and public housing agencies have the resources to help these families. In the past, a lack of coordination between these agencies has often prevented families from finding the housing assistance they need. Today's complex family situations urgently require collaboration between agencies. Providing safe, affordable housing to families can be an effective and inexpensive way to support family stability and prevent the placement of children in foster care.

This manual will offer suggestions to help child welfare agencies and housing agencies* build strong collaborations to improve services for families in both systems. It will demonstrate successful models for linking subsidized housing with supportive social services. It will also suggest ways to bring health care providers into the partnership with child welfare and housing, so families have access to the primary care they need as well as "wraparound" services, such as mental health and substance abuse counseling.

This manual describes various methods of prioritizing federal housing subsidies for families identified by a child welfare agency, including the Family Unification Program. It also highlights innovative programs that several states have implemented to house and support families. The manual should help communities across the country provide safe, stable, subsidized housing to families in the child welfare system. Federal legislation currently pending will send communities fewer regulations and fewer dollars to implement these social programs. Collaboration between agencies will be more important than ever to maximize these dollars and ensure effective program delivery.

Benefits of Collaboration between Housing Agencies and Child Welfare Agencies

Housing Problems and Their Impact on Family Stability

In communities across the United States, families struggle to find safe, decent, and affordable housing. The struggle is especially difficult for low-income families, who are often forced to choose among bad options. For example, many poor families spend a huge percentage of their income on housing, leaving little for food and other necessities; others share overcrowded housing or live in substandard housing that poses health risks to parents and children.

---

* The term *housing agency* (or HA) denotes a public or private nonprofit agency responsible for administering federal, state, and local housing programs, including Section 8, and public housing.

Subsidized housing is a scarce resource in tremendous demand. The U.S. Conference of Mayors' *Status Report on Hunger and Homelessness in America's Cities: 1995* documents this growing scarcity. The report collected data from 29 cities, and found that in 1995, requests for assisted housing by low income families and individuals increased in 73% of the survey cities and remained the same in 27%. No city reported a decrease in such requests. It follows from this unmet housing need that a growing number of families are becoming homeless. Families with children made up 36.5% of the homeless population in the cities surveyed for the 1995 mayors' report. In 1985, the same survey found that families with children were 27% of the homeless population.

Child welfare agencies* are increasingly confronted with families' housing problems. A study by the American Public Welfare Association [APWA 1995] offers the first national statistics on the prevalence of homelessness and inadequate housing in families involved with the child welfare system. APWA surveyed 270 local and 42 state public child welfare agencies.

The agencies answering the question reported that some 26.4% of children entering care were affected by either homelessness or inadequate housing, among other factors. Twenty-five percent of children unable to return home from foster care were affected by homelessness or inadequate housing combined with other factors. There was considerable variance in the impact of housing issues on families, depending on the size of the agency reporting. Small agencies estimated that 19.2% of children entering care were affected by housing issues, while large agencies estimated that 40.3% of children entering care were affected by inadequate housing or homelessness.

Two composite stories illustrate the links between child welfare and families' housing problems.

> The Jones family has been struggling but surviving on the edge of poverty for many years. When Mr. Jones lost his construction job and eventually left the family, Mrs. Jones and her three children were thrown into crisis. Her part-time job could not support her family, and after several months of paying only partial rent, they were evicted from their apartment. They stayed temporarily with several relatives, but no one was able to house them permanently.
>
> The constant moves caused the Jones children to miss a lot of school. The school sent the child welfare agency out to investigate. They told Mrs. Jones that if she could not acquire stable housing for her children immediately, they were at imminent risk of being placed in foster care because of neglect. Although the family was on the waiting list at their local housing agency for Section 8 housing, the wait for assistance was over two years. Mrs. Jones's small income made it impossible for her to afford a decent apartment without assistance. Her three children were placed in two different foster homes.

*   *   *

* We use the term *child welfare agency* to refer to a public agency responsible for children who have been abused and neglected. Many of the strategies discussed would also be effective for private agencies.

The two Green children were placed in foster care because of suspected neglect. Before her children were placed in care, Ms. Green had a part-time job and received AFDC. When the children entered care, the AFDC assistance stopped. She was unable to afford her apartment, and moved in with friends. Ms. Green has attended parenting classes, visited her children frequently, and fulfilled all the other requirements of her child welfare service plan. The child welfare agency is ready to return the Green children to their mother, but the Juvenile Court is reluctant to release them until she has her own place to live. The children are stranded in foster care.

Statistics indicate that these scenarios are common.

- In St. Louis, Missouri, in 1993, 17 children every month—204 during the course of the year—were placed in foster care primarily due to inadequate housing. Over two-thirds of the children referred to the juvenile court with inadequate housing as a primary problem were placed in out-of-home care because no housing resources were available.

- The public child welfare agency in Contra Costa County, California, estimated in 1993 that 30% of its families could be stabilized or reunified if housing assistance were available.

- A New Jersey study found that homelessness was an underlying condition for 42% of the families with children in the state child welfare system, and a causal factor for 25% of the city of Newark's foster care placements [Zalkind 1988].

- A report issued by the National Black Child Development Institute found that in one-third of all cases, inadequate housing or homelessness was the main factor leading to foster care placement, and a major obstacle to the child returning home [NBCDI 1988].

Collaboration Benefits Everyone

Collaboration between child welfare agencies and public housing agencies can benefit families and agencies alike.

Families in crisis benefit by having the comprehensive housing and support services they need delivered in a coordinated way. Child welfare agencies benefit by gaining access to valuable housing resources, and are able to reserve scarce foster care placements for children who need them because of abuse or willful neglect.

The Family Unification Program, discussed in detail below, is only one example. Many child welfare agencies have found that working with their local housing agency has allowed them to secure Section 8 certificates and public housing slots for families they serve. Other child welfare agencies have helped to establish state and locally supported housing subsidies for their clients through new state legislation.

Housing agencies also gain through collaboration with child welfare agencies. The supportive services and case management the child welfare agency provides can stabilize families and make them more reliable tenants. The child welfare agency can assist the housing agency when families are in crisis, and can sometimes avert costly and difficult evictions. In some communities, the child welfare agency has helped the housing agency build linkages to a number of other community agencies.

A lack of collaboration in the past has hurt families and been expensive for communities. If the housing needs of families in the child welfare system go unmet, children may be unnecessarily placed in foster care, or be delayed in reuniting with their parents. Unnecessary foster care placements—including those that could be prevented if a family received housing assistance—are very costly. In 1993, the average total federal cost of placing one child in foster care for one year was $10,833 [CWLA 1995]. The CWLA FUP survey found that these families have an average of 2.7 children. Foster care for each family in the FUP program, then, costs an average of $29,249 per year. By contrast, providing an entire family with housing assistance through the federal Section 8 program costs an average of $8,900.

Beyond the financial costs, foster care placements can be devastating to the emotional lives of children and parents. The damage caused by separation can take years to repair. The coordination of housing assistance and child welfare services is especially valuable because it can prevent or shorten family separations and help build stronger, safer homes for children.

Child Welfare Agency Basics

The child welfare system is charged with the protection of children who have been abused or neglected and those who are at risk of abuse or neglect. Public and private child welfare agencies work with children and their families to protect children, promote family stability, support families' strengths, intervene when necessary to ensure children's safety and well-being, and address social conditions that negatively affect children.

Child welfare agencies provide a wide range of services, including family preservation and support programs, which try to prevent separation of children and parents by providing intensive services; child protection services, which address the needs of children who have been abused and neglected; out-of-home care, including several kinds of foster care, for children who are deemed temporarily unsafe at home; and adoption for children who cannot be cared for by their birth parents [Liederman 1995].

Housing Agency Basics

Public housing agencies develop, own, and manage rental housing for low-income families and individuals. These independent agencies are governed by local boards; the programs they manage are funded and regulated by federal, state, and local governments.

Many public housing agencies manage public housing developments for families, individuals, the elderly, and the disabled. Approximately 50% of public housing residents nationwide are either elderly or disabled. Local housing agencies also administer a federally subsidized private rental housing program called Section 8. In both public housing and the Section 8 certificate program, the federal government subsidizes the difference between 30% of a family's gross income, which the family pays in rent, and the actual rent. Families and individuals in public housing live in apartments owned and managed by the public housing agency. Families who participate in the Section 8 program live in apartments available on the private rental market.

Challenges to Housing/Child Welfare Collaboration

Different institutional criteria and regulations pose a challenge to collaboration between housing agencies and child welfare agencies. Recognizing the basic differences can help communities meet that challenge and build strong, collaborative relationships.

Although each child welfare agency and each public housing agency is unique, there are some major differences between the two kinds of agencies.

Client access to services

Child welfare agencies (CWA) work with families who are referred to them because of suspected abuse or neglect. Although some families ask child welfare agencies for help, most families do not choose to get involved with these agencies. Child welfare agencies are committed to keeping children safe. They do this by strengthening families whenever possible, but also by removing children when necessary. Families can be resistant to CWA services out of fear of losing their children. CWA workers must walk a fine line between being supporters of families and enforcers of regulations. Current legislation provides these investigative and protective services to children as entitlements. Families of all income levels are eligible to receive child welfare agency services. Welfare reform proposals under consideration by Congress could change the funding for these services, possibly making them less available.

Housing assistance is a very limited resource; demand far outstrips supply. Housing agencies work only with very low-income families, and only with those families who request assistance. Most housing agencies maintain long waiting lists for assistance, and serve families on a first-come, first-served basis. Families are required to meet multiple criteria, in addition to income measures, to actually receive housing assistance.

Funding and regulations

Child welfare agencies are supported by federal, state, and local funds. Under federal regulations, as of mid-1996, low-income children are entitled to foster care services. Current federal regulations guide the way that cases are handled, requiring, for example, that cases be reviewed every six months. Rules governing the investigation of child abuse and the specific services provided to each family vary from state to state. Passage of proposed welfare reform legislation could change both the funding and the regulations for these services. These changes will most likely result in less funding and fewer federal regulations, with more decisions being left to state administrations.

Housing agencies are supported by federal funds and governed by federal statutes and regulations. Many derive additional funds from local public and private sources. Federal housing subsidies are not entitlements. Multiple criteria other than need determine which families receive housing assistance. Pending federal housing legislation could shift greater responsibility to local agencies in determining both what services are available and who will receive housing assistance.

These institutional differences between agencies create widely varying attitudes and expectations among staff members. Child welfare workers tend to get involved in many aspects of their client family's problems and needs. Every family that enters the child welfare system has a right to certain services. A case worker strives to serve a family's needs as comprehensively as possible.

Housing agencies distribute and manage scarce housing resources for entire communities of low-income people. They must require that a family has certain strengths before they receive this assistance. Their services are not distributed simply on the basis of need. Workers in both kinds of agencies, engaging in a collaboration, will benefit considerably by understanding and accepting the different orientations of the services they provide. The better each can understand the goals and limitations of the other's agency, the more effective and less frustrating the collaboration will be.

Beyond cultural differences, collaboration between child welfare and housing can also be hindered by overworked staffs and limited resources. Many housing agencies are swamped by requests for assistance. It is not uncommon for large housing agencies to maintain waiting lists of over 10,000 households. Most child welfare agencies are similarly overloaded. CWLA program standards recommend that child welfare social workers maintain caseloads no larger than 15 families, but workers across the country are commonly responsible for 30, 50, or even 70 cases at a time.

Collaboration between agencies is crucial to provide much-needed services to families. Open-minded communication and sharing of resources between agencies is increasingly important as changes in federal legislation devolve the responsibility for programs to local agencies. These program changes do not come easily. It is the nature of bureaucracies to get stuck in familiar patterns of operations. Program collaboration requires a commitment to change from all the people involved. Child welfare agencies and housing agencies in many communities have developed these strong links, enabling thousands of families to provide safe and stable homes for their children. This manual will outline the steps to creating these partnerships in your own community.

References

American Public Welfare Association. (December 1995). *Housing and foster care: Results of a national survey*. Washington, DC: Author.

Child Welfare League of America. (1995). *Child abuse and neglect: A look at the states*. Washington, DC: Author.

Liederman, David S. (1995). Child Welfare Overview. In Edwards, Richard L., Ed., *The Encyclopedia of Social Work*, 19th Edition. Washington, DC: NASW Press.

National Black Child Development Institute, Inc. (1988). *Who will care when parents can't? A study of black children in foster care*. Washington, DC: Author.

The United States Conference of Mayors. (1995, December). *A status report on hunger and homelessness in America's cities, 1995: A 29-city survey*. Washington, DC: Author.

Zalkind, C. (1988). *Splintered lives: A report on decision making for children in foster care*. Newark, NJ: Association for Children of New Jersey.

Part One

Support for Families: Housing/Child Welfare Collaborations

The following sections describe resources now available to help families and children stay together when housing problems threaten them with separation or delayed reunification.

xisting Housing Resources

The Section 8 Program

Section 8 is a federally-funded program that provides housing assistance to low-income families, primarily by subsidizing private market rents. In most communities, assistance is initially provided only to families with incomes below 50% of the community's median income. A family may make more than 50% of median income after initial lease-up for continued residence in Section 8 housing.

Once a family or an individual is leased-up in Section 8 housing, they have significant tenant rights under Section 8 regulations. Changes in family composition, including a child's departure for foster care or failing to be returned, are not grounds for the termination of Section 8 assistance. This holds true even if the family was awarded the certificate to allow the children to be reunited with the family. Careful screening of families before their referral for these housing assistance programs is crucial if the program is to be a success and families are going to stay together.

Families with Section 8 certificates look for housing in the private rental market. When they find an appropriate apartment whose landlord is willing to participate in the Section 8 program, two agreements are executed. The first is a lease between the tenant and the landlord. The other outlines the relationship between the landlord and the public housing agency. Participating families pay 30% of their income toward the rent in the private market. Federal funds, administered by the local public housing agency, subsidize the difference between the tenant's contribution and the actual rent, which can be up to 40% of the Fair Market Rent.

The Fair Market Rent (FMR) is determined annually by HUD for each apartment size in a community, and represents the average rent paid. Section 8 certificates are limited to use in apartments and houses that rent for no more than 40% of FMR. A family with a certificate cannot pay more than 30% of its income toward rent. There is no limit to the full rent of apartments or houses when a tenant uses a voucher, but the HUD contribution does not increase as the rent goes up.

Through FY 1995, families have been required to meet federal preference criteria in addition to income limits in order to receive housing assistance. Federal legislation dropped the federal preference requirements from housing programs for FY 1996. It is unclear whether these preference requirements will be reinstated after FY '96 or not. A lot depends on the presidential and congressional elections of 1996. Currently, each local housing agency can determine its own preference system or can remain with the federal preferences it has been working under.

Previously, federal preferences were extended to families living in substandard housing, those who were involuntarily displaced, and those spending more than 50% of their income for housing. (See Appendix I for a detailed discussion of federal preferences.) Under the old regulations, a public housing agency had to provide at least 90% of its Section 8 certificates to families who qualified for at least one federal preference. Most used 100%. The preferences essentially functioned as eligibility criteria.

The current legislative changes open this process up, so that local agencies can determine who will receive housing assistance. This represents an excellent opportunity for housing agencies to reexamine the needs of families involved with the child welfare system and prioritize them for service. Child welfare agency staff and local child advocates can take advantage of these new opportunities by making sure that housing agency staff are aware of the housing needs of these families. The change in federal legislation makes this a perfect time to begin a collaboration between local housing agencies and child welfare agencies.

Accessing This Resource for Families

Committing Section 8 Funding to Child Welfare Families

Any community can designate Section 8 resources for families identified by the child welfare agency who need housing assistance to bring their children home from foster care or to prevent their initial placement in care.

🏠 Communities that are doing away with the federal preferences and establishing their own local priorities can use the above eligibility criteria as a preference for service.

🏠 Communities that are maintaining the use of federal preferences can establish a *ranking preference* for the above defined families to be selected from the total pool of families meeting a federal preference. A housing agency may establish a ranking preference for as large a portion of its Section 8 resources as it chooses. This is an extremely effective strategy for serving these vulnerable families if an agency is maintaining the federal preferences.

The state of Massachusetts created a ranking preference for CWA-identified families in 1993. The state had been a Family Unification Program (FUP) grantee in FY 1992 (see page 7 for FUP details). When the agency did not receive an additional allocation of FUP funds in FY 1993, administrators developed this ranking preference to expand their program. The Division of Housing and Community Development, Massachusetts Department of Economic Development (formerly the Executive Office of Communities and Development, or EOCD) with the support of the state Department of Social Services, submitted an amended administrative plan to HUD designating this ranking preference. (See Appendix B.) HUD approved EOCD's request to designate 75 of its regular Section 8 vouchers for families that fit the CWA criteria and also qualified for a federal preference. ❤*

This process is even simpler under the new regulations. Housing agencies no longer need to wait for HUD approval to implement preference criteria. The dispersement of Section 8 certificates can be determined locally through the Consolidated Planning process. The participation of both public and private service agencies in this planning process is crucial to ensure that CWA families are included in the Consolidated Plan. This planning process is designed to increase the voice of the local community in determining the allocation of housing and development resources. All new local preferences for Section 8 need to be approved through this planning process. See page 5 for details.

Establishing Local Preferences for Section 8 Certificates

In communities no longer using federal preferences, all selection criteria are now local preferences. Previously, under the federal preferences, only 10% of an agency's Section 8 certificates and vouchers could be used for families and individuals who did not fulfill a federal preference. Local agencies maintaining federal preferences can now establish any breakdown between federal and local preferences that they choose. They can stay with the 90/10 split, go to 50/50, or choose any other combination that is approved by the community through the planning process.

Local preferences are designed to give the local agency an opportunity to serve any housing needs of its community that did not fit into the federal preferences. Without federal preferences, local designations will determine the use of all housing assistance. This change in regulations is meant to encourage local agencies to fully assess the housing needs in their community and design programs to address them.

For example, housing agencies, child welfare agencies, and others can collaborate to develop a local preference that gives a high priority to families identified by the child welfare agency as needing housing assistance to bring their children home from foster care or to prevent their initial placement in alternative care. The housing agency needs to amend its administrative plan to indicate that "families

The ❤ symbol indicates that a contact for this program is listed in Appendix A.

whose children are unable to return from foster care, or are at risk of placement into foster care, primarily due to lack of adequate housing" qualify for a local preference.

🏠 The Housing Opportunities Commission of Montgomery County, Maryland, gives a local preference on its housing waiting list to families identified by the County Department of Health and Human Services as 1) families whose lack of adequate housing may result in foster care placement or delay in family reunification or 2) homeless families housed in shelters or hotels at county expense or families facing homelessness due to termination of time-limited government rent subsidies. These local preferences, in addition to the local preference for families living in substandard housing, which these identified families will also receive, makes it possible for Montgomery County to serve this population with Section 8 or public housing. The repeal of the federal preference requirements in FY 1996 allows Montgomery County to increase the number of certificates used for local preferences like these. Local preference had been linked to 10% of total Section 8; housing authorities are now free to extend this preference to any proportion of its housing certificates, up to 100%. ❤

HUD's Consolidated Plan

This is a planning process that all child welfare agencies and community advocates need to be active in. This process and the resulting document determine HUD's spending priorities for the community. Needs highlighted in the Consolidated Plan stand a good chance of being funded. Needs not included in the plan stand little chance of receiving funds or attention from the department. All new local preferences for Section 8 housing need to be approved through the Consolidated Plan process. The housing needs of CWA families have to be introduced in this process if they are to receive funds.

In 1995, HUD published its Consolidated Plan Regulations. This one planning process replaces the Comprehensive Housing Affordability Strategy (CHAS) and the planning documents for the Community Development Block Grant, Emergency Shelter Grant (ESG), HOME, and Housing Opportunities for People with AIDS (HOPWA).

The consolidated plan is HUD's answer to complaints from communities across the country about the many different planning processes they had to use to apply for programs in the past. HUD's intent in establishing a new planning process is to promote citizen participation and develop local priority needs and objectives, coordinate statutory requirements to minimize the federal intrusion into state and local planning activities and simplify the funding process, promote the development of an action plan that provides a basis for assessing performance, and encourage consultation with public and private agencies to identify shared needs and solutions [Housing Development Report 1994].

The consolidated plan serves as a planning document for a given jurisdiction (state, county, city or town), an application for federal funds under HUD's formula grant programs, a strategy for carrying out HUD programs, and an action plan that provides a basis for assessing performance. The plan must be submitted in a format prescribed by HUD, including forms and narratives, or in another format jointly agreed on by HUD and the jurisdiction. It must provide a housing and homeless needs assessment; a housing market analysis; strategies, priority needs and objectives; an action plan; certifications; and a description of monitoring efforts.

Assessing the needs of families and setting priorities for community initiatives clearly demands participation of the agencies which are responsible for the well-being of children. Citizen and agency participation is a vital part of the consolidated planning process. In the development of the plan, jurisdictions must consult with public and private agencies that provide assisted housing, health services and social services. Detailed citizen participation plans must be developed by states or localities. Each plan must encourage the broadest participation, emphasizing the involvement of low-income residents and neighborhoods. Jurisdictions must encourage the participation of residents of public and assisted housing developments.

After the initial plan is written a period of at least 30 days must be allowed for the comments of citizens and local government. At least two public hearings must be held per year, conveniently timed for those who will benefit from program funds, accessible to the disabled, and adequately publicized. These hearings address housing and community development needs, development of proposed activities, and program performance. At least one of these hearings is held before the proposed consolidated plan is published for comment.

This process is clearly constructed to the advantage of community members and agencies that serve vulnerable families, children and individuals. It is crucial that child welfare agencies are active partners with their local governments in the development of these consolidated plans. The information in these plans determines which programs in a community are funded by HUD and which ones are not.

The provisions in this description of the consolidated plan are mandated by federal law. If you want further information about this process see the HUD Consolidated Plan regulation, CFR 24 part 91.

How to Do It

- Become well acquainted with the local government office that is heading-up the consolidated plan process. This will most likely be the Mayor or County Commissioner's Office.

- Be sure to have a vocal representative involved in the planning process early on that will ensure the housing needs of CWA families are carefully articulated.

- Encourage other agencies concerned with the welfare of families and children to play an active role in the consolidated plan process.

The Family Unification Program

Much of what has been learned about establishing specific housing programs for families identified by the child welfare agency has grown out of experience with the federal Family Unification Program (FUP). This limited federal demonstration program first drew congressional attention to the plight of families separated by homelessness and inadequate housing. Although FUP presently remains limited to only 16 states, the techniques and lessons learned are useful for all communities developing programs to house these vulnerable families.

In 1990, Congress established the Family Unification Program (FUP) as part of the Cranston-Gonzalez National Affordable Housing Act—42 USC §1437(x). (Appropriations legislation for P.L. 102-139 and P.L. 102-389 contain related information.) FUP provides Section 8 housing assistance to families who are eligible for Section 8 *and* whose children are at imminent risk of placement into foster care, or delayed in returning home from foster care, when housing problems are a *primary*—though not necessarily the only—factor. The federal statute allows FUP certificates to be used to prevent initial foster care placements and to facilitate the reunification of children with their families.

The History of the Family Unification Program

Since the initial passage of the Family Unification Program in 1990, over 6,000 Section 8 certificates have been issued. From FY 1992 through FY 1995, funding was provided for five-year Section 8 certificates. The FY 1996 appropriation is for two-year Section 8 certificates. Both five-year and two-year certificates can be renewed if funds are available. So far the certificates have housed an estimated 22,600 children and parents.

Table 1. The Funding History of the FUP

Fiscal year	Appropriations	Eligible states	Communities granted funds
FY 1992	$50 million	11 states*	62
FY 1993	$75 million	16 states**	30
FY 1994	$63.5 million	16 states	32
FY 1995	$73 million	16 states	36
FY 1996	$28.5 million	16 states	42

* California, Florida, Maryland, Massachusetts, Michigan, Missouri, New Jersey, New York, Ohio, Pennsylvania, and Texas. (P.L. 102-139)

** FY 1992 states and Georgia, Illinois, Minnesota, North Carolina, and Virginia. (P.L. 102-389)

The long-term future of the FUP is unclear. Congress has voted to eliminate virtually all new funding for Section 8 housing, but despite the deep cuts in other housing programs, there has been strong support for the Family Unification Program. In the Continuing Omnibus Budget for FY 1996, Congress set aside $400 million for Section 8 certificates and vouchers to be used for specified purposes. The Family Unification Program is specifically mentioned as an allowable use for these certificates.

In the Notice of Funding Availability (NOFA) dated May 2, 1996, HUD made up to $32 million available for FUP. In September 1996, HUD headquarters drew from the pool of applicant agencies that passed the baseline criteria evaluated by the HUD field offices. Forty-two agencies have been awarded funds for the FY 1996 FUP.

Congress passed a housing appropriations bill for FY 1997 in late September 1996. Once again, FUP activities will be paid out of a special Section 8 set-aside. HUD has decided not to issue a new NOFA for these funds in 1997. Instead, HUD will fund the remaining applicant agencies that were not selected in the lottery for FY 1996 funding. This ensures broader application of FUP funds and prevents the administration burden of another NOFA. Provided there is funding for FUP in 1998 and beyond, there will be future NOFAs and opportunities for new agencies to participate in this federal program.

FUP is available only to families in the 16 states selected by Congress and HUD: California, Florida, Georgia, Illinois, Massachusetts, Maryland, Michigan, Minnesota, Missouri, New York, New Jersey, North Carolina, Ohio, Pennsylvania, Texas and Virginia.

The original statue for FUP indicates that this program will be funded in all fifty states after the initial demonstration program. Unfortunately, cuts in HUD's funding from Congress have prevented growth in the program. Appropriations in FY 1996 will be limited to the sixteen states that have participated in FUP since 1993. The process followed by the local agencies in applying to HUD for funds will remain the same as well. The additional Section 8 funds awarded to FUP communities is the only thing that distinguishes them from non-eligible communities.

The Family Unification Program Application Process

Housing and child welfare agencies in the 16 designated states have the opportunity to apply for FUP specific funds from HUD each year that an appropriation is made. HUD releases a Notice of Funding Availability (NOFA) when the funds are cleared through Congress and HUD for distribution. (See Appendix C for the FY 1996 FUP NOFA, published in the Federal Register for May 2, 1996.) CWLA distributes the FUP NOFA to all previous FUP applicants and other interested agencies.

Close collaboration between agencies begins with the FUP application process. There should be an initial series of meetings for all involved staff members at the two agencies. These meetings can also include local activists and service providers who are involved in the process. There is a period of six to eight weeks between the release of the NOFA and the date the applications are due into the local area HUD offices. The application requires the housing agency to meet certain criteria in order to be eligible for FUP funds. A completed application includes a report written by the local child welfare agency describing the effect of inadequate housing and homelessness on the separation of families in the community. (The report can be prepared by a city, county, or state child welfare agency to correspond to a city, county, or state housing agency.) The participating child welfare agency is also required to commit sufficient staff time and resources to identify and refer eligible families to the housing agency (HA) and to assist in the program's implementation.

FUP requires ongoing collaboration between the child welfare agency and the public housing agency. In brief, the child welfare agency is responsible for identifying and referring FUP-eligible families to the public housing agency; the public housing agency is responsible for administering the FUP certificates as part of its Section 8 program. Locally initiated programs that serve this same population of families operate the same way. After the federal FUP application process and the awarding of funds, both grantee and non-grantee communities can establish programs using the same steps and procedures, which are outlined in this manual.

Establishing Section 8 Priorities for CWA Families

All collaborative programs require strong commitment by the staff of involved agencies. In the past, federal funds have worked as a catalyst for these efforts, but now more than ever, local resources and initiatives are at the core of effective housing support for families.

Table of Tasks

This table lays out the major tasks involved in implementing a Section 8 housing program for families identified by the child welfare agency. The steps outlined in this table apply to both federally funded FUP and locally designed programs. The table also shows who is responsible for each step. Note that for many of the steps there is an X in both agency columns. Collaboration and shared responsibility are vital to these programs.

Each numbered task is discussed in detail in the text that follows the table. The statistics cited in the breakdown come from a telephone survey of FY 1992 FUP grantee agencies conducted by CWLA in 1995. For the complete results and the survey instrument, see Appendix E.

Breakdown of Tasks

1. Hold initial meetings and brainstorm.

Face to face meetings between the staff members of both agencies involved with the collaborative effort are very important, especially in the beginning. These meetings will set the tone for the collaboration and encourage personal commitment to the program by those who participate.

Child Welfare Agency	**Table 2. Tasks in Housing/Child Welfare Collaboration** X *Indicates primary or shared responsibility.*	Housing Agency
X	1. Hold initial meetings to address housing needs of CWA families, build relationships, and brainstorm on program possibilities.	X
X	2. Appoint program liaisons who will hold primary responsibility for the program at their agency.	X
X	3. Assess housing situation of each family at intake and facilitate getting family on HA waiting lists whenever appropriate.	
X	4. If community is federal FUP eligible, apply for HUD funds through NOFA.	X
	5. If community is not FUP eligible, designate CWA families with a local Section 8 preference, commit state/local housing funds for families, or create other access to assistance for families.	X
X	6. Conduct cross-training of staff on each agency's regulations and expectations for a collaborative program.	X
X	7. Write and implement a memorandum of understanding and program protocols.	X
X	8. Develop an internal tool for screening families being considered for housing assistance.	
X	9. Develop a written process to refer and track families between agencies. This also facilitates annual evaluation of the program.	X
X	10. Have each family sign a release form to allow the sharing of information between agencies before referral.	
	11. Verify income, federal preference (if applicable), and debt history status of each family referred for housing.	X
	12. Conduct Section 8 orientation with each accepted family, issue certificate, and provide housing search assistance.	X
X	13. Develop follow-up service plan for each family housed through the program and provide case management for at least 6 months after lease-up.	
X	14. Facilitate and encourage participation in the Family Self-Sufficiency (FSS) program after receiving housing.	X
X	15. Contact liaison at partner agency if any problems arise or there are changes in family status, income, program eligibility, etc.	X
	16. Contact CWA prior to termination of assistance with a family or and any time a housing certificate becomes available.	X
	17. Perform annual recertifications of each family's eligibility for continued assistance under Section 8.	X

In a survey of the FY 1992 FUP grantee agencies, 38% of child welfare agencies reported having some contact with a housing agency before the FUP. However, for the majority, 62% of the child welfare agencies surveyed, FUP was their first and only contact with their community housing agency. FUP creates relationships between agencies and individuals where none have existed before. In many communities, FUP has served as the catalyst for collaborative relationships and multiple shared programs.

The federal FUP statute designates housing assistance for families unable to get their children back from foster care or at imminent risk of losing their children to care primarily because they lack adequate housing. Discussions among agency staff can lead to a further refining of the population to be served by either the federal FUP or a locally designed program.

At the initiative of the child welfare agency, the program can concentrate solely on reunifying families that have been separated for over six months. Or the agencies can choose to focus on the prevention of family breakup by providing housing assistance to families already receiving Family Preservation Services. The state of Massachusetts has concentrated its FUP resources on women and children who are coming out of domestic violence shelters with no place to go.

These local decisions are best made cooperatively between agencies and at the outset of the collaborative process.

2. Appoint liaisons from each agency.

This is a key step. The liaisons should have authority within their respective agencies to make necessary decisions about the program, and should be in frequent contact.

- In San Jose, California, FUP was most effective when the liaisons were in contact about the program and specific cases as often as every few days. ❤

- In the FY 1992 FUP survey, 100% of the child welfare agencies reported having a liaison at the public housing agency. Some 93% of the housing agencies surveyed reported knowing their liaison at the child welfare agency.

A strong collaboration requires continuous contact between the agency liaisons and others involved in the collaborative effort.

- In Atlanta, Georgia, collaborating staff of the housing agency and the child welfare agency meet monthly to discuss individual cases. The meetings focus on families involved with both systems and work to prevent evictions and foster care placements by combining agency resources. Frequent phone contact between meetings helps resolve problems that arise. ❤

- In Baltimore County, Maryland, the assigned liaisons from the child welfare agency and the housing agency meet once a week. Their offices are located in the same building so they have the advantage of proximity. They speak frequently by phone between the weekly meetings. The housing agency liaison keeps her child welfare counterpart informed about the status of each case. The child welfare liaison communicates with the social workers on her staff to help families find new homes and achieve stability. ❤

3. Assess housing situation of families at intake. (CWA)

Intake forms can be amended to include questions about a family's housing situation. Greater awareness of the housing issues of every family in the CWA caseload from their initial contact will help the CWA and the HA address these needs. Child welfare workers have often not been aware of their client's housing needs until a crisis occurs. Better knowledge, earlier, can help avert these crises and increase awareness of the community's housing concerns. Even before a specific program is established for these families, they can benefit by applying for assistance at the local housing agency. Getting families on the HA waiting list will help them obtain services and also bring attention to the need for assistance in a community. Community needs that go unrecorded stand little chance of being addressed.

4. Apply for FUP funds from HUD.

If your community is eligible, refer to page 8 for detailed coverage of the federal application process.

5. Designate a local preference for CWA families.

Refer to page 4 for a detailed discussion of local preferences for CWA families.

6. Cross-train staff of involved agencies.

Agencies should conduct training sessions for child welfare workers and housing agency staff members (including supervisors) who will be involved with the collaborative housing program.

Collaborations often require that people change the way they do their jobs. Training staff of all of the agencies involved is critical. Wherever possible, agencies should work to train each other's staffs. Public housing agencies can offer training about the Section 8 program to social workers in the child welfare agency.

🏠 In St. Louis, Missouri, the child welfare agency and the public housing agency, along with other agencies, have convened day-long training conferences, sharing information about the resources, rules, and regulations of the various agencies. ❤

🏠 Orange County Department of Social Services, California, in conjunction with the housing agency, holds annual trainings for CWA case workers on housing and collaborative approaches to accessing it for clients. ❤

7. Develop a written memorandum of understanding (MOU).

This document will establish the roles and responsibilities for each agency. A good MOU will address all relevant aspects of administering an FUP, including the screening of families, referrals between agencies, follow-up services, and program evaluation. All the program steps outlined in the above table should be addressed in the MOU. This document is your road map for this child welfare and housing program. The care you take in developing it will pay off during the implementation of the program. The MOU can also be amended and updated as the program progresses and activities are refined. (CWLA's model MOU is included as Appendix E.)

In CWLA's survey of FY 1992 grantees, 60% of the sites reported having a Memorandum of Understanding. Some 20% of the respondents didn't know if their agency had an MOU. This most likely speaks to the fact that some first-year agencies may write an MOU, but fail to use it as a guide while implementing the program. Active use of MOUs has improved each year of the federal FUP.

It is important to define roles and expectations within as well as between agencies. In addition to the MOU, it is useful for the collaborators to write program protocols that outline the responsibilities of workers in each agency.

> 🏠 The New Jersey Department of Community Affairs (DCA—the state housing agency) and the Department of Human Services, Division of Youth and Family Services (DYFS) developed a Family Unification Program Protocol that explains program eligibility and lays out a detailed referral process for workers at both DYFS and DCA. This document also includes specific time lines and a process for conflict resolution between agencies. ❤ (See Appendix F for a copy of the protocol.)

Written materials that explain how a collaborative program functions in a community can answer many concerns about the program, can help expand it into other parts of the community, and can assist other communities who wish to replicate its success.

8. Develop a screening tool.

Your MOU should include written criteria for determining which families will be served by these Section 8 certificates. Be sure the workers of both agencies understand the requirements of the program for families. Once a family is leased-up in Section 8 assisted housing, the lease can only be terminated if its terms are violated. Separation of family members is not grounds for terminating the housing assistance, even if assistance was received specifically to bring the family together. The most successful FUP families are those who have shown the ability to be self-reliant and the motivation to take on new and challenging responsibilities.

About half of the child welfare agencies established priority groups for the FUP program. Approximately 14% focused on using FUP to prevent foster care placements, while 30% prioritized bringing children home from care with the FUP. However, this is not how the actual allotment of certificates was distributed. Considerably more children were prevented from going into care than were returned home due to FUP. This most likely speaks to the difficulty of reuniting a family after a period of separation.

Certain questions should be asked before any family is referred for a subsidized housing program. Here are some examples.

1. Has the family ever maintained a home independently before? Do the parents know how to run a household?

2. Do the parents show initiative throughout the process? Are they demonstrating that they want this responsibility?

3. Does the family have anything in their past they may prevent them from being eligible for housing assistance—a past debt or damage claim with the housing agency, a felony conviction, or recent substance abuse?

4. Are there adequate support services available to meet this family's needs?

🏠 In St. Louis, Missouri, representatives of the child welfare agency, the juvenile court, the housing agency, and several local service providers jointly developed an assessment tool to identify families who would benefit from and succeed in the FUP program. A selection team was established to choose among those families found eligible through the assessment process. (A copy of the assessment tool is attached as Appendix H.) Unfortunately, this tool has not been used with the FUP because St. Louis has received no certificates since the first year. However, it has helped guide the selection of families for local and state housing efforts. ❤

Experience with FUP has shown that families receiving housing assistance and being reunited after a child has been in foster care often require significant supportive services. CWA workers need to assess the agency's and the community's ability to provide these services before referring them for housing. All aspects of a family's situation must be considered by the CWA before making a referral for housing. A family must be truly ready to be reunited before the responsibility of independent housing is placed on them.

9. *Establish a clear process for referrals between agencies.*

This will require written referral forms that help both agencies track cases. Federal FUP grantees no longer have to clear the HA waiting lists before accepting referrals from the CWA. They cross-check their waiting list with a list of active cases from the CWA, while also accepting referrals. Locally designed programs need to address these waiting list issues early on in the process.

Annual program evaluation should also be considered when these referral forms are being written. Referral forms are included in Appendix E, the sample MOU.

🏠 Experience with the federal FUP has shown that nearly all the referrals should come from the CWA to the HA. The survey of FY 1992 grantees found that many sites originally experimented with multiple referral strategies, but 90% settled on a process in which almost all referrals originate with the child welfare agency.

🏠 The HA can ask clients to contact their CWA worker if they have one, but it is the CWA that will evaluate the status of the family and judge their appropriateness for housing assistance.

There needs to be an interagency agreement about how the families will be referred and how records will be kept. Most FUP grantees have found that referring a few families at a time is more efficient for everyone than sending over a long list of families at once. The child welfare liaison should review families case workers identify for the program. Those that appear to meet the criteria should be referred to the HA liaison. If this housing assistance is intended to intervene in a crisis and prevent family separation, families should be referred only when this assistance is immediately appropriate for them.

🏠 The San Jose child welfare agency developed an internal form that is filled out by social workers who believe their clients are eligible for FUP. The forms are given to the child welfare liaison. The CWA and HA together developed a two-part interagency form. If the liaison agrees that the family is appropriate she fills out part of the form and sends it on to the housing agency liaison. The public housing agency fills out the other half and sends it back to the child welfare agency. This process keeps the child welfare agency informed of the progress of the housing application for each family. ❤ (A copy of the form is attached as Appendix H.)

When to refer families is an important decision, especially when dealing with families who will be reunified through the program. In Illinois, they've found that it is helpful to refer a family 60 to 90 days before a child is due to be released from foster care. This gives the parent(s) sufficient time to locate housing before the children are returned.

10. Obtain a release of information form. (CWA)

This form is signed by each family before they are referred to the HA for housing assistance. Confidentially rules require the CWA to receive this clearance before sharing information about a family with other agencies. One simple form can authorize all necessary communication between the agencies regarding a specific family throughout their participation in housing program.

11. Verify family's eligibility for Section 8 assistance. (HA)

In addition to meeting the eligibility criteria of the collaborative program, each family must qualify for Section 8 assistance. The public housing agency will verify that a family's income falls below its cutoff, usually 50% of the area's median income for initial occupancy of units.

If the HA is maintaining the use of federal preferences, the family also has to qualify for either a federal or a local preference to receive assistance. For FY 1996, Congress has lifted the use of federal preferences in housing assistance. Local agencies now have significant freedom in determining who will receive assistance, although they also have the option of keeping the federal preferences intact. See Appendix I for information on the federal preferences and how they may be used in this new environment.

Local housing agencies also check the credit and legal histories of potential tenants. Local regulations vary, but a felony conviction will often preclude a family from receiving housing assistance. Any existing debt with the housing agency also has to be cleared before a new certificate can be issued. In many FUP grantee communities, the CWA and the HA have worked together to help families pay off their debts before receiving housing. Flexibility and cooperation on the part of both agencies and families is crucial to the success of these programs.

12. Conduct orientation and issues certificate. (HA)

This is standard procedure for any Section 8 program. An orientation meeting is required before a family can be issued a certificate. The family needs to bring multiple documents to verify their income and other factors. The length and depth of the orientation training varies between agencies.

In the FY 1992 FUP grantees survey, 86% of the housing agencies reported they provided some kind of housing search assistance to families in the first year of FUP. Housing assistance in some agencies is limited to giving families a list of available properties in the area. Other agencies offer more substantive help, such as negotiating with landlords or helping families move once a lease is signed.

13. Provide support services and case management. (CWA)

In the FY 1992 FUP survey, 90% of the child welfare agencies reported providing ongoing case management to families in the FUP. CWA case workers provide critical guidance and support to families throughout their transition to permanent housing.

> In St. Petersburg, Florida, CWA case workers help families collect all the necessary documents and attend the Section 8 orientation meeting with each family.

Families often need considerable support while they are looking for a suitable apartment or house. Initially, they have 60 days after their certificate is issued to find housing. In some areas it may very difficult to locate housing in 60 days, even in the best conditions. Many families referred through these programs do not have adequate transportation or child care and may not know the housing in the area well. HAs have the option of extending a family's search period an additional 60 days (to a total of 120 days). CWA case workers can improve a family's situation considerably by helping them locate suitable housing in a stable neighborhood.

The first six months that a family is in their new housing is a sensitive transition period. Experience with the FUP has shown that CWA case management throughout this period helps secure the family and link them to community resources. Each family should be assessed individually, and their needs met as closely as possible. The commitment of agency resources to these families is critical. In many cases, both undergraduate and graduate student interns can provide excellent support for these families without straining the department's overburdened workers.

> In St. Louis, Missouri, graduate social work student interns at the child welfare agency helped families search for housing once they received certificates, and continued to work with them until their housing situa-

tion was stable. This assistance included helping families with the nuts and bolts of new housing—finding furniture, negotiating with the landlord about repairs, and linking the family to community agencies. The students also conducted an evaluation of the program and the families' experiences within it. ❤

14. Facilitate participation in the Family Self-Sufficiency Program (FSS).

As has already been stated, follow-up support services are critical for CWA families who receive housing through these programs. Because resources at both agencies are limited, creating links between existing programs is important. Extensive services and case management are available to families through the Family Self-Sufficiency Program of the Department of Housing and Urban Development (HUD). The goal of FSS is to give families the skills and experience they need to be off public assistance within five to seven years. For a complete discussion of FSS and links to CWA/HA collaborative programs see pages 51-55 [change].

15. Maintain communication between agencies.

Section 8 certificates are a scarce commodity and a valuable resource to families and communities. On-going communication between the CWA and HA will ensure they are efficiently managed and that families enjoy the full benefits of these collaborative programs. Changes in family status (a marriage, a new baby or a child going into family foster care) can affect a family's housing assistance. Changes or problems in a family that affect their housing situation should be relayed to the housing agency. Similarly, if the HA has problems with a family they should let the CWA know. Small concerns can grow into major problems if they are not addressed right away. These communications also build understanding and relationships between the agencies that improve the quality of services for all the families the two systems serve.

16. Contact CWA before terminating assistance and when certificates become available. (HA)

Families can leave their subsidized housing for a number of reasons. They may move out of the area, and can usually transfer their housing assistance to the agency in their new area. If the receiving agency "absorbs" this family, the certificate returns to the original housing agency. This process varies considerably. Some receiving agencies will not absorb transferring families, and the original housing agency remains responsible for the family's assistance in their new community. CWAs should be clear about the procedures in their area.

Occasionally families will have to be terminated from Section 8 for non-payment of rent or other lease violations. The HA should notify the CWA if a family is heading in this direction before it becomes to late to intervene. If the family works with the two agencies, most evictions can be avoided. If a family is terminated from the program, the certificate comes back to the HA and is issued to a new CWA referral. Ongoing communication between agencies during this process will expedite assistance to a new family.

17. Perform annual recertification of each family in the program. (HA)

Local housing agencies must recertify every family receiving Section 8 assistance every year. During this recertification the assistance will be adjusted for changes in family composition and income. Families may move to a different unit at this time and still stay on Section 8 assistance. Until recently, Section 8 certificates were issued for five years and were renewable after that. However in the last several years HUD has issued two-year certificates that will be renewable if funds are available.

ousing Program Evaluation

Evaluation is an essential part of program implementation. A well designed evaluation should be able to measure the effectiveness of the program in meeting its stated goals and indicate areas that need refining and improvement. In this time of shrinking budgets, a strong evaluation can help a program remain funded and possibly even expand. The federal FUP has been implemented as a demonstration, which makes program evaluation crucial for future funding in this area.

🏠 The original Family Unification Program statute indicates that HUD will conduct an evaluation of this program. The five Notices of Funding Availability (NOFAs) that have been released require each applicant agency to agree to participate in this evaluation. When it became apparent that HUD had no evaluation planned, CWLA secured funds through the Robert Wood Johnson Foundation to conduct an evaluation of the FY 1993 FUP grantees. CWLA contracted with the Vanderbilt University Institute for Policy Studies to conduct the evaluation. During the course of this two-year project, the Annie E. Casey Foundation provided financial support for a CWLA phone survey of the grantee agencies from the FY 1992 FUP.

Both these evaluation efforts were designed to identify who was being referred, accepted, and housed with the Section 8 certificates. They also addressed process issues, such as design of the referral process, support services provided and lessons learned from the implementation of the program.

Frequent evaluation can help collaborative programs stay on track and build support for the collaboration among policymakers and funding agencies. Ultimately, programs should be evaluated in terms of their goals—e.g. improving access to housing assistance for families in the child welfare system—and should not be held responsible for resolving fundamental problems—for example, lack of affordable housing and persistent poverty.

Below are listed a few selected results from each of these studies. These findings support the recommended activities for implementing child welfare and housing collaborations that were covered earlier in this manual. These surveys, along with national and regional meetings, multiple technical assistance visits, and ongoing phone contact with sites, have created the body of knowledge that is shared here.

The FY 1993 study, by Vanderbilt University, is still in progress, and final results are not expected before late 1996. See Appendix J for a fuller description of their preliminary results. See Appendix D for full results of the CWLA FY 1992 grantees study, along with the survey instrument.

Early Success of FUP

Child welfare workers from California to Massachusetts have found the Family Unification Program "the best resource we've ever had to serve and protect families."

One mother who benefited from the program wrote:

> "A year ago, my four children and I were living in inadequate housing. We were overcrowded and often had to be out on the street for several hours each day. Thanks to the referral to the FUP we were able to get, through Section 8, adequate housing in one to two weeks.
>
> Had we been forced to wait the usual 6 months to 2 years for housing, I believe I would have lost my children to foster care and had a nervous breakdown myself."

The following are a few examples of the program's success:

- In Los Angeles, 20 Section 8 certificates have housed and reunited 127 people, including 100 children who would have likely been placed in foster care if FUP assistance had not been available.

- In Cincinnati, all 21 families who received FUP assistance are stable and together more than two years later. The program has kept 58 children out of foster care.

- In St. Louis, FUP has brought the Jones children home. Ms. Jones had worked two jobs after her husband left the family. But when her health failed she could not work anymore, and the family started to move every few months in search of an affordable home. Her three children, ages 9, 11, & 13, were placed in foster care when their last apartment was condemned. Once the children were in care, the court would not release them until Ms. Jones found an acceptable place to live. Thanks to the FUP program, the family has now lived in the same apartment for two years and the children have completed two full years at one school—the longest period of stability they have ever experienced.

Evaluations of 1992 and 1993 FUP Grantees

All data referring to the 1992 program are from CWLA's telephone survey of FUP grantee agencies, conducted in 1995. (See Appendix D for a complete analysis of the 1992 data.) All data referring to the 1993 program are from Vanderbilt's program evaluation, which is still in progress. All 1993 data are preliminary and reflect only those families on whom data is complete.

Table 3. Basic Statistics

FY 1992

Children housed with 827 FUP certificates	2,223
Foster care placements avoided	1,275
Children returned home from foster care	869

FY 1993

Families housed as of 12/95:	955
Female-headed families housed	85%
Average age of primary parent	31 years
Race/ethnicity of primary parent:	
Caucasian	33%
African American	48%
Hispanic	17%
Average # of children in family	2.6 children
Families with more than 3 children	23%
Families with a child under 1 year	18%
Families with a child under 3 years	52%

Providing Comprehensive Support for Families

Most families involved with the child welfare system benefit from continued supportive services during and beyond the housing search process. FUP grantees have learned that ongoing services from the child welfare agency, the housing agency, and other community service providers is crucial to families' success. This kind of support benefits agencies and families alike by reducing the number of families whose children come back into foster care because of problems with the new housing arrangement.

Child welfare agency activities that promote successful families include:

🏠 careful screening and selection of families who can benefit from housing assistance;

🏠 helping families gather and submit necessary documentation for housing application;

🏠 providing all or part of a security deposit and/or helping families locate other sources of funds for move-in costs;

🏠 helping families search for housing and negotiate with landlords; and

🏠 committing resources for support services to assist families after they find housing.

Services That Help Families Stabilize

Ongoing support services for families who receive housing assistance through FUP and other programs are critical. Many families involved with the child welfare system face major challenges in their lives, including unemployment, domestic violence, substance abuse, and disabilities. Housing is a crucial first step. Once a family is housed, other supports can help them resolve ongoing issues so they can stay together in stable housing.

🏠 In San Jose, the child welfare agency linked all of the families participating in the FUP program to a Family Resource Center. The Family Resource Centers offer families a wide range of support services and educational opportunities, including counseling and programs that address home maintenance skills and budgeting. ❤

🏠 In St. Louis, the child welfare agency supervised a social work student who provided intensive, daily support to families with FUP certificates. She helped families negotiate with landlords, find furniture, and develop ties to their new communities. Both graduate and undergraduate student interns can be an excellent resource for FUP agencies in providing support services to families after they are housed. ❤

🏠 In New Jersey, a district office of the Division of Children, Youth, and Families is exploring the use of Federally Qualified Health Centers (FQHC) to provide various types of health and mental health services to troubled families. See page 36 for details on FQHCs and the financial benefits of partnering with these centers. ❤

🏠 The state of Illinois actively uses the FUP Advisory Committee to follow up with families. The Department of Children and Family Services (DCFS) provides follow-up services for six months, after which members of the Advisory Committee obtain additional services to meet each family's needs. These services are coordinated by student interns at DCFS after the CWA case is closed. ❤

🏠 In Contra Costa County, California, the Health Services Department is looking into the possibilities of Federally Qualified Health Center (FQHC) reimbursement and other sources to establish a Family Maintenance Organization (FMO), which will help families in the child welfare system, as well as other families, gain access to a broad range of wraparound services. The FMO would be part of a county-run health maintenance organization in which many Medicaid families are already enrolled. ❤ (See pages 36–40 for a detailed discussion of FQHC.)

Accessing Support through Family Self-Sufficiency

The Family Self-Sufficiency program (FSS), operated by HUD, can help child welfare agencies and housing agencies provide a range of critical services to families after they've been leased-up in Section 8 or public housing. FSS creates a bridge between CWA case management and complete independence for a family. FSS provides the services and skills training for a family's progress toward a self-sufficient life.

FSS Basics

Family Self-Sufficiency is designed to enable recipients of housing assistance to become self-sufficient in 5 to 7 years (extended, in some cases, to 10 years). A "self-sufficient" family in this context is one who does not receive AFDC, Food Stamps, Medicaid, or means-tested SSI. A family that graduates from FSS can still receive rental assistance.

From 1992 to 1995, housing agencies were required to enroll one family in FSS for each new Section 8 or public housing unit the housing agency receives from HUD. For example, if the Anytown Housing Authority is awarded 30 Section 8 certificates, it must place 30 families in FSS. It does not have to be the same 30 families who use the new certificates. The housing agency can fill FSS slots with families who already live in assisted housing and are interested in enrolling in a self-sufficiency program. Legislative changes in 1995 have removed the FSS mandate for housing agencies. FSS, however, is still the only HUD program that makes comprehensive services and individual case management available for families.

The housing agency is responsible for referring FSS participants for the services they need. Each FSS program creates a Coordinating Committee of local service providers to meet the needs of participant families. This committee represents many local public and private nonprofit agencies that provide job training, education, child care, health care, substance abuse treatment, legal services, parenting classes, counseling, and transportation assistance. FSS does not include funds to pay for the provision of these necessary services. Service provision relies on the partnerships built through the coordinating committee and the resources of each community.

FSS benefits families in several ways. The agency initiatives that are coordinated through FSS provide families access to support services and training opportunities that might otherwise be very hard to obtain. Continued participation in FSS also builds the family an escrow (savings) account that they can use upon graduation from the program.

Housing subsidy programs are often criticized because of the way the rent payment changes as the family's income increase. In all federal housing subsidy programs, each time a family's income increases, their subsidy is reduced and they are required to pay more rent for their unit. This often feels like punishment to a struggling family. It may even be a disincentive for families to increase their earned income, since it makes saving money impossible.

In the FSS program, a family is still required to pay more rent as their income goes up, but the housing agency deposits an amount equal to the increase in their rent into their escrow account each month. In this way, the family builds savings while gaining skills and attaining self-sufficiency. When the family graduates from public assistance they already have savings that can be used for a down payment on a home, for security deposits, for advanced education or for any other financial needs the family identifies. A family forfeits their escrow account if they drop out of the program before graduating.

🏠 The New Jersey Department of Community Affairs (DCA) reports that 46% of the families who entered FSS since 1993 are currently employed and near self-sufficiency. They attribute this high rate of success to the work of nine dedicated social workers who work with the FSS participants. DCA uses substantial Section 8 administrative funds to support the social workers. FSS families have been referred to jobs, educational programs, vocational training, internships, and volunteer work. ❤

Linking CWA Families to FSS

Linking families housed through CWA/HA collaborations will work best when the housing agency has hired an FSS coordinator to work with the families. HUD offers some housing agencies limited funds to pay for FSS coordinators, whose role is to help families develop a self-sufficiency plan and to link them with the services they need. Most large housing agencies do not receive additional funds for a coordinator, but are expect to use general funds to cover this position.

🏠 In Ithaca, New York, 11 of the 22 families in the FUP program are also participating in the FSS program. Most other FUP sites have had little participation of FUP families in FSS. The high rate of participation in Ithaca is due to the persistent hard work of the FSS coordinator, who also runs the FUP. She has dedicated herself to helping FUP families succeed in FSS. ❤

Participation in the FSS program is often a significant challenge for CWA families, particularly in communities without a strong FSS coordinator. FSS programs need to be carefully designed so that families' needs can be met in a comprehensive manner. Families involved with FUP and CWA are often in the midst of several crises when they are first referred for housing assistance. Their participation in FSS has to be designed appropriately to their needs if they are going to be successful. Steps should be taken slowly. For example, the entire first year in the program can be dedicated to improving parenting skills and providing support services to help the family reunify and stabilize as a unit. FSS goals should be realistic in both substance and timing.

Careful consideration needs to be given to a family's future prospects before they enter FSS. Some families, such as those with serious physical or mental disabilities, may never be self-sufficient. These families are not good candidates for FSS. FSS is a valuable program for families when it is constructed to meet their needs as they progress and is based on a realistic vision of the family's potential.

FSS is one of the few national models that exist for the many welfare-to-work programs currently being designed as a result of both federal and state welfare reform. The long-term commitment of both agencies and families, and the emphasis on comprehensive services—not just job placement—are vital to the success of FSS.

How to Do It

🏠 Housing agencies should hire or assign FSS coordinators who can work closely with FSS participants, including interested FUP families. The coordinators can help families develop appropriate self-sufficiency plans and find needed services.

🏠 Child welfare agencies should educate themselves about the FSS, and should work with housing staff to identify families, including FUP participants, who would benefit from FSS participation. (Former child welfare workers are highly effective coordinators in some housing agencies.)

🏠 Child welfare agencies should get involved with the FSS coordinating committee in every housing agency that has an FSS program. The CWA and HA should work together to provide case management services to CWA clients who enroll in FSS.

🏠 Child welfare and housing agencies (working together) can be strong advocates for local programs that provide adequate time and resources to enable families to achieve self-sufficiency.

Unfortunately, in the interest of cutting costs, many state and local programs are shortening time frames and reducing available resources. In this environment, realistic goals and careful case management will be more important than ever.

Innovative State and Local Efforts

Communities around the country have identified a number of strategies that can link families in the child welfare system with housing assistance and other supportive services. Some of these strategies are specific to Section 8 housing, while others involve a range of different funding sources.

In the past, these local initiatives were generally small programs developed to complement federally funded programs. Political changes both in Washington and at the state level are shifting responsibility for all types of social programs to city and county administrations. Today, and more so into the future, local initiatives and the commitment of local/state resources will be crucial to the provision of basic support services to families. Effective service delivery will not be possible without the kinds of local collaborations described in this section. CWLA is available to assist communities in developing cross-systems initiatives. See Appendix A for details.

Expanded Federal Preferences

In FY 1996, FY 1997, and for the foreseeable future, local housing agencies have the option of continuing to use the federal preferences for housing or repealing them and setting up their own preference structure. For more details on the federal preferences see Appendix I. The following section describes a practice used with the federal preferences in place to allow a greater number of CWA families to qualify for assistance.

Any program established to meet the needs of CWA families should consider "doubled up" families who are separated or at risk of separation because of overcrowded housing conditions. After many years of advocacy, CWLA and the FUP sites have been successful in convincing HUD to address the needs of these families.

The FY 1996 FUP NOFA expands the program criteria to include them. This program regulation applies to all Family Unification program sites. It is a major victory for agencies struggling to provide truly adequate housing for the families they serve.

Many child welfare agencies have identified families who would benefit from the FUP program but cannot participate because they do not qualify for a Section 8 housing federal preference. These families are now included in the federal FUP, and no further program changes are necessary to serve them. In communities without FUP funding, public housing agencies may expand the definition of a preference by submitting an amended administrative plan to HUD. Once submitted the plan may be acted on. HUD approval is implied unless HUD specifically contacts the HA with a problem.

🏠 Massachusetts successfully used this strategy to assist families living in overcrowded conditions. The Department of Social Services (DSS) was reluctant to release children from foster care into severely crowded housing and wanted to secure FUP assistance for those families. Although families living in "substandard housing" are eligible for a federal preference and were therefore good candidates for FUP, HUD's definition of substandard housing addressed issues such as running water, inside plumbing, and heat—overcrowding did not qualify. These "doubled-up" families are well known to most CWA workers. Finding stable housing for these families has been a consistent problem.

In order to extend FUP assistance to these families, the Massachusetts Executive Office of Communities and Development (EOCD) and DDS together developed a new definition of "lack of adequate housing." This new definition includes families whose housing "does not provide adequate space for the family to be reunified according to the Department of Social Services occupancy standards." EOCD submitted to HUD an amendment to its administrative plan; HUD approved the amendment. (Appendix K) ❤

Housing Subsidies Funded with Child Welfare Dollars

Several states have established housing subsidy programs funded with child welfare dollars. These programs were created to address the problems of families whose children were ready to return home but were stranded in foster care because the family lacked adequate housing. Child welfare agencies and state legislatures recognized that subsidizing a family's housing is significantly cheaper—and more humane—than continuing a foster care placement for a child ready to return home.

🏠 In 1989, Arizona established the Housing Assistance Program (HAP). The state uses child welfare funds to provide a rent subsidy of up to $300 per month for six months. The subsidies are available to families whose children cannot come home from foster care because the family lacks adequate housing. In the state's fiscal year 1995, $104,454 was expended to return 225 children to 100 families. The program, administered by the Department of Economic Security, saved the state $192,826 in foster care costs that year. ❤

In 1991, the Illinois Department of Children and Family Services (DCFS) established a Housing Assistance Program (HAP) made up of private agencies that provide housing advocacy services to families who are part of the class created by the settlement in *Norman v. McDonald*, a class action suit against the state filed on behalf of families whose children were delayed in returning home from foster care primarily because of their families' struggle with poverty. The federal consent decree entered in March of 1991 required the Department to assist families whose children are at risk of placement or not being returned to them due to inadequate food, clothing, shelter, and/or environmental neglect. HAP provides referrals to emergency shelters, assistance in locating permanent housing, assistance applying for income assistance, linkage to other community resources, and follow-up services. HAP also provides one-time cash assistance for rent and move-in expenses. There are currently 21 HAP agencies throughout the state. ❤

In 1988, New York State created Preventive Housing Services. The program *requires* local social service departments to provide housing assistance to families for whom the lack of adequate housing is the primary factor blocking *reunification* with a child in out-of-home care. In 1991, a demonstration program in a select number local social service departments began providing the same assistance to prevent family breakups. To qualify for this assistance, families must be at *imminent risk* of losing their children to out-of-home care, due primarily to inadequate housing. Additional risk factors must be present—inadequate housing alone is not grounds for the placement of children in out-of-home care in New York and most other states. In 1995, Preventive Housing Services—designed to *prevent* the placement of children in foster care— was extended permanently as an optional program to all local social service districts in the state. Preventive Housing Service cash grants, either for family reunification or the prevention of placement, are used primarily as monthly rent subsidies not to exceed $300.00 per month. This cash assistance may cover other essentials such as one-time payment of arrearages, brokers' or finders' fees, security deposits, and essentials repairs. Preventive Housing Service grants are limited to a maximum of 36 months or a total value of $10,800 per family. ❤

In 1994, Missouri enacted child welfare reform legislation that provides housing subsidies for families who need assistance to prevent the placement of their children in substitute care or to reunify their families. These funds support housing subsidies up to the local fair market rent (FMR) for a maximum of six months. During this six-month period, case workers help families move toward self-sufficiency. Funds can be used to clear past debts to landlords, housing agencies, or utility companies. The child welfare moneys can also pay security deposits. This program has been in operation since February 1995. As of June 1996 it had served 457 families. ❤

Overcoming Barriers to Housing CWA Families

Using CWA funds for clients in debt

Some families eligible for FUP assistance have back debts to the housing agency, usually for utilities or for damage done to a previous unit. Housing agencies will not provide a family with Section 8 assistance until the debt has been cleared. Child welfare agencies need to work closely with families and housing agencies to ensure that back debts do not disqualify families who are otherwise eligible for FUP and other housing assistance.

- In Pinellas County, Florida, the child welfare agency used its flexible funds to help families clear housing and utility debts.

- In San Jose, California, the child welfare agency and the housing agency negotiated payment schedules on a case by case basis that allowed families to move into new units while paying off their debts. The child welfare agency provided some funds to families through its family preservation program. ❤

- The state of Missouri has appropriated a separate stream of money to the Department of Social Services, Division of Family Services (DFS) for a Crisis Intervention Fund. Each DFS office contracts with a government agency (university, city or county administration, etc.) to access the funds for needy families. In St. Louis City the agency contracted with the Mayor's office. These funds have paid for rent and back rent, water heaters and furnace repairs, utility bills, beds and other basic furniture, as well as work and school supplies. Partnership with local government has enabled DFS to receive needed funds in a week rather than the month or more required when going through state offices. ❤

Other sources of funds include Community Action Agency programs, nonprofit housing organizations, churches, and other community groups.

Additional Collaborations between Local Child Welfare Agencies and Housing Agencies

- In 1994, an Atlanta child welfare agency supervisor went to visit one of his clients. The client had a three-month old baby on a monitor due to health problems. This family had just been evicted from their public housing unit. The supervisor tried, unsuccessfully, to intervene with the public housing agency. From this experience grew a strong collaboration.

  Child welfare and housing agency staff now meet monthly to discuss individual cases and policy issues. Families sign releases so that the two agencies can discuss cases without breaching confidentiality. Child welfare agency staff members often go to public housing developments to meet with families and housing agency staff and resolve problems that arise. The housing agency now notifies the child welfare agency before any of its clients are evicted. Child welfare agency staff works with the family and the housing agency to help the family retain its housing. ♥

🏠 In St. Louis, a multidisciplinary group of professionals concerned about homelessness and inadequate housing has been meeting since 1991. The group includes representatives of the St. Louis Housing Authority, the Missouri Division of Family Services, the Missouri Department of Mental Health's Division of Alcohol and Drug Abuse, the George Warren Brown School of Social Work, Citizens for Missouri's Children (a private advocacy organization), Legal Services of Eastern Missouri, and the Salvation Army. This group has worked together on developing FUP applications and linking services for families selected to participate in the program for several years. This group was critical in the introduction and establishment of the state housing assistance legislation that passed in 1994.

How to Do It

🏠 All HA employees should understand that the temporary absence of a child does not affect a family's ability to apply or qualify for housing assistance.

🏠 Housing and child welfare agencies should develop a mechanism for communicating about families who might benefit from the "temporary placement" policy.

🏠 Child welfare agencies should encourage housing agencies in their communities to adopt this policy and/or ensure that it is being practiced. The guidance in Appendix L may provide useful background material.

The group continues to work on creating new housing resources for vulnerable families involved in the child welfare system. For example, they work with current and potential Section 8 landlords and the managers of project-based Section 8 to improve the access and services available to families. The Department of Mental Health is working with the group on a project-based Section 8 complex to provide transitional housing for families before they receive permanent housing. They have also begun recruiting new Section 8 landlords by advertising in local papers and setting-up a phone line to answer questions and link potential landlords to the city and county housing agencies. ♥

Incorporating Regulations on the "Temporary Absence of a Child"

The National Affordable Housing Act states that children in "temporary" foster care should be counted as part of a family unit for purposes of determining a family's eligibility for housing assistance. (Housing agencies establish their own definitions of temporary.) Parents awaiting their children's return home from foster care can apply for housing assistance—and for a unit big enough for the entire family—before their children have been returned to their custody.

Most housing agencies have already incorporated this policy into their administration plans. Child welfare agencies and others should verify this in their own community and be sure that this policy is being practiced in the Section 8 program. Appendix L is an example of HUD guidance to housing agencies about this policy.

The new law means that housing agencies must accept applications from families whose children are in foster care. Housing agencies and child welfare agencies can work together to develop a protocol for working with these families. For example, a housing agency can agree to process applications from families whose social workers will certify that the children are in a temporary placement, and that housing is needed before the children can return to their parents.

This policy also helps families living in subsidized housing—including FUP, regular Section 8 and public housing—whose children are placed into foster care. A family participating in FUP *does not* lose their Section 8 housing if one or all of their children are placed in foster care. Although the family received this housing assistance to enable the reunification of their family, once they are in their Section 8 housing they have all the same rights as other Section 8 tenants.

Housing agencies and child welfare agencies can work together to establish a time frame that is considered "temporary placement" for children. Six months is often used as the cut-off for temporary placement, but this should be determined with local needs and conditions in mind. Once a placement has been determined to be long-term, the housing agency can require the remaining family members to move into a smaller unit. When the children are ready to be returned home the housing agency is required to increase the family's subsidy to allow them to move into a unit large enough to accommodate the entire family. Because this procedure takes considerable time and work for both agencies and the involved family, it is important that everyone work together and moving the family is avoided whenever possible.

References for Part One

42 USC 1437(x). Appropriations legislation P.L. 102-139 and P.L. 102-389 contain related information.

U.S. Department of Housing and Urban Development. (1994, August). Housing Development Report, Current Developments. Washington, DC: HUD.

U.S. Department of Housing and Urban Development. (1995, January). Consolidated Submission for Community Planning and Development Programs; Final Rule. 24 CFR Part 91, et al. Washington, DC: HUD.

U.S. Department of Housing and Urban Development. (1995, July). Preliminary Analysis of FY 1996 House Subcommittee Appropriations Bill. Washington, DC: HUD.

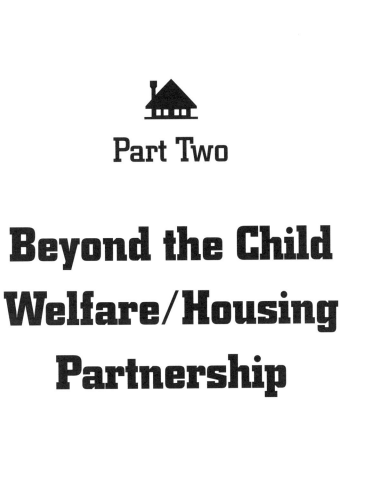

Part Two

Beyond the Child Welfare/Housing Partnership

Finding and Funding Primary Health Care and Mental Health Services

The Child Welfare League of America has encouraged and supported agencies participating in the Family Unification Program to expand their collaborative network to include not only housing agencies, but health care providers as well. The Federally Qualified Health Center (FQHC) program, a relatively new Medicaid and Medicare funding mechanism, is a key to child welfare/health care partnerships. By establishing a partnership with a Federally Qualified Health Center, a child welfare agency can gain access to essential services for families, funded largely by Medicaid, including primary health care and mental health, substance abuse, and case management services.

The FUP experience has demonstrated that for families in many communities, even when lack of appropriate housing appears to be the major barrier to family unification, access to housing is not by itself a sufficient remedy. In fact, for some families, the move into decent, stable housing actually precipitates a crisis. Problems that appeared manageable while a family was struggling with immediate issues of shelter and survival intensify soon after the family is housed, threatening its ability to keep the housing and to stay together. For these families, housing is essential, but it is not enough. They need continued supportive services.

Child welfare agencies in every state spend a large proportion of their discretionary dollars to purchase or provide medical and mental health services for the most vulnerable children and families in their care. Unfortunately, as budgets tighten, these services are often abandoned, even though providers understand that short-term disinvestment in support services will mean a far greater cost to the system in the long run.

Still, in today's volatile health care environment, there are opportunities for child welfare agencies to establish productive, mutually beneficial partnerships with health care organizations. These health care partners have the resources and the motivation to provide the services children and families in the child welfare system need. They can offer a cost-effective way to provide essential, high quality follow-up care to families who have received Section 8 certificates and other families involved with the child welfare agency.

FQHC Basics

The FQHC program is a generous Medicaid and Medicare reimbursement mechanism that compensates some health care providers on the basis of the actual cost of delivering services. Unlike the traditional "fee-for-service" Medicaid reimbursement mechanism, which sets a specific payment for each type of service, Medicaid pays Federally Qualified Health Centers a global rate based on their annual cost reports. Since the actual cost of providing services is almost always higher than Medicaid fee-for-service payments, Federally Qualified Health Centers generate substantially more Medicaid revenue than most other providers.

The per-visit rate covers the direct cost of services by certain practitioners, including physicians, physician assistants, nurse practitioners, clinical psychologists, and licensed clinical social workers. The rate also covers reasonable administrative and overhead expenses, and it is adjusted every year on the basis of the FQHC's actual costs for that year.

When services are provided directly by one of the "billable" practitioners listed above, each face-to-face encounter with a Medicaid beneficiary generates a Medicaid bill, whether that service is provided at the provider's clinic facility or in the client's home. Service provided by a FQHC staff member who is supervised by a physician or one of the other listed providers (for example, a community health worker or certified substance abuse counselor) may not be viewed as a billable visit, but these services can often be partially reimbursed by Medicaid. All of the reasonable and allowable costs of providing FQHC services as defined in the regulations are included in the formula that establishes each entity's Medicaid rate.

FQHC funding is available only to health care agencies that meet specific federal criteria. Some entities are automatically eligible for this enhanced reimbursement, including those receiving federal grants as migrant farm worker programs, community health centers, and providers of health care for the homeless. (These programs are known as "329," "330," or "340" programs, in reference to the sections of the Public Health Service Act under which they funded.)

If a community-based nonprofit or public health care provider does not receive federal funding under one of these programs, it may still qualify as an FQHC by demonstrating that it meets all the requirements for such funding. Entities that qualify by this latter method are known as "lookalike" Federally Qualified Health Centers. Most of the communities participating in the Family Unification Program are currently served by a Federally Qualified Health Center or by an agency that is a potential "lookalike."

FQHC funds a broad spectrum of services, including primary medical care provided by a physician, physician assistant, or nurse practitioner. In addition, one of the significant innovations of the FQHC entitlement is that it requires state Medicaid agencies to pay for the services of licensed clinical social workers and clinical psychologists when these services are provided by a Federally Qualified Health Center. Other services may also be funded, depending on each state's Medicaid plan. FQHC can cover comprehensive primary health care, mental health counseling, drug and alcohol abuse services, case management, children's and adult dentistry, nutrition, health education, and other services.

Benefits of FQHC/Child Welfare Collaboration

In most communities, resources for primary health care, mental health care, substance abuse treatment, and other such services fall far short of the need. The lack of appropriate support services often forces child welfare agencies to keep cases open much longer than they would if those services were available in the community.

A child welfare/FQHC partnership will help a child welfare agency provide families with the services they need. The child welfare partner will be able to refer families from its caseload to a clinic-based case manager who has access to a broad array of necessary services.

Troubled and fragile families represent an enormous cost to the community agencies that are our society's real safety net—child welfare agencies, juvenile and criminal justice systems, homeless shelters, and residential treatment programs. Unless vulnerable families get the help they need to address their long-term, underlying problems, they are unlikely to achieve the stability it takes to maintain themselves in permanent housing and stay out of the "system."

The FQHC program was designed to encourage community health centers to expand their services to underserved populations. The program provides genuine financial incentives to agencies that serve additional Medicaid beneficiaries. Because the FQHC program pays these providers their actual cost of serving Medicaid clients, an agency that increases its services to these clients also increases the share of its total budget funded by Medicaid. In most child welfare agencies, 80% to 100% of the families served are eligible for Medicaid. In most communities, child welfare agencies should be able to find one or more health centers that are highly motivated to enter into collaborative relationships that benefit both partners.

FQHC and Health Care Reform

Many health center administrators are concerned about the future of the FQHC program—and of their core grant program (e.g., Health Care for the Homeless)—in whatever system emerges from the present federal effort to reduce Medicaid and Medicare expenditures. Congress and the Administration have both signaled a general commitment to continue support for community health providers, including Federally Qualified Health Centers, at least during a several-year transition to whatever federal- or state-run health insurance system for the poor finally emerges from the political process.

Although systemic health insurance reform failed at the federal level, virtually every state has initiated its own version of Medicaid reform. Most have adopted some form of managed care. The states are mirroring the changes in the private insurance marketplace—states and employers alike have found that they can gain some control over the escalating cost of health care by negotiating deals with managed care organizations.

As the states move toward Medicaid managed care, many providers who historically have been uninterested in the Medicaid population are now opening clinics in poor neighborhoods and actively competing with the community-based and public health care "safety net" providers for a share of this market. FQHCs have some advantages in this newly competitive arena. The capacity of Federally Qualified Health Centers to offer a broad array of supportive services funded at a higher level than the services of competing providers will help them compete in this new arena.

Child welfare agencies bring a valuable resource—Medicaid referrals—to their collaborations with health care providers. Some child welfare agencies have been courted by several health care organizations seeking these referrals. Sometimes, child welfare agencies find better services and a higher degree of motivation in a non-FQHC provider (a teaching hospital or a mainstream managed care organization) than in an FQHC. Several states, including Tennessee and Oregon, have received waivers from the U.S. Department of Health and Human Services (HHS) exempting them from the requirement to fund FQHC services as part of their Medicaid-managed health care reform efforts. It appears that states will not be routinely excused from the FQHC mandate, however, and will at least have to show how state reform efforts will ensure appropriate care for the vulnerable populations Federally Qualified Health Centers serve. Even in states that have received federal permission to eliminate the FQHC program, there are motivated providers competing in the Medicaid market place who will be interested in serving child welfare families.

Barriers to FQHC/Child Welfare Collaboration

States vary considerably in the array of services included in their Medicaid plans and in their method of calculating reimbursement to FQHCs. Even when there are several Federally Qualified Health Centers within a single city, they will vary in their capacity for growth and collaboration. The development of effective partnerships often requires organizations to move beyond historical isolation or competition with one another and to build new, mutually beneficial working relationships. Each of these partnerships must be shaped by local conditions and by the rules established in the state's Medicaid plan. Reaching agreement between a primary health care provider, firmly grounded in the medical model, and a social service provider—even on the meaning of the term *case management*—tests all of the participants' flexibility and sense of humor. However, the gains for families and for the agencies that serve them can be substantial.

Resources to Support FQHC/Child Welfare Collaboration

The National Clearinghouse on Primary Care Information publishes a free annual

Directory of Bureau of Primary Health Care-supported Primary Care Centers, which lists all of the FQHCs in the United States. Copies are available by calling 703/821-8955. The Child Welfare League of America also offers ongoing technical assistance to agencies seeking health care partners. See Appendix A for details.

The Collaborative Process

In the past few years, numerous child welfare agencies and housing agencies have worked to establish collaborative relationships in an atmosphere of limited funding and unlimited work. The benefits of these efforts often extend beyond the original project to positively impact many program areas the agencies have in common.

The challenge is in making these coordinated programs a reality and incorporating collaborative practices into many aspects of agency activity. The segregated services that are created by individual agencies and their separate funding streams do not fully address the way people live their lives and the kinds of support they need. Collaboration between agencies helps bridge the gap between what a client actually needs and what a particular agency can offer.

Collaborative efforts can create new, dynamic service possibilities previously unavailable from any single agency. Speaking about the FUP program—which cannot operate without close collaboration—one child welfare worker in New Jersey said, "This is the best resource we've ever had to truly serve families."

This section offers some practical suggestions to facilitate collaboration. We encourage readers to pick and choose among the strategies that sound most useful, to revise them to fit local needs, and to try different approaches until a collaboration takes hold.

The First Step: Getting the Right People to the Table

A collaboration is a set of relationships among people. Collaboration among agencies—in this case, child welfare agencies, public housing agencies, and community health care providers—is, in fact, the sum of relationships among people in those agencies.

Experience has demonstrated that child welfare/housing collaborations will work best if the people involved share these characteristics:

🏠 an understanding of the links between housing assistance and family stability for families involved with the child welfare system;

🏠 a commitment to meet the needs of the most vulnerable families; to do "whatever it takes";

🏠 a willingness to learn about the other agency's mission, concerns, programs, rules, and restrictions;

🏠 a commitment to working through problems as they arise, including a commitment to case-by-case collaborations about the needs of specific families;

🏠 a willingness to be flexible and to search for solutions when rules or past practice pose problems—and not to get stuck at "we've never done it that way before."

We have also seen that collaboration works best if the commitment extends throughout the agencies—from the agency directors, who can authorize needed revisions in rules and regulations, to the intake and direct service workers, who deal with families every day.

🏠 In San Jose, California, a strong FUP program was built with the cooperation of the Deputy Director of the Social Services Agency and the Director of the Section 8 Program. The day-to-day collaboration fell to the child welfare agency's Family Preservation Specialist and the housing agency's Community Services Coordinator, who now speak almost daily on the phone. ❤

🏠 In Massachusetts, the child welfare agency developed an innovative program in collaboration with four nonprofit housing agencies responsible for administering the Section 8 program. The directors of the child welfare and housing agencies offered strong support for the collaboration. This collaboration facilitated the operation of the FUP program and the commitment of state resources to serve child welfare-involved families in need of housing assistance. (See page 3.) ❤

Communicating

In order to communicate effectively, staff members need to address their pre-conceived notions about their partner agency. Common stereotypes held include "Housing agencies are bound by rigid rules and they don't really care about the welfare of the families they serve," and "Child welfare families are too much trouble and not good tenants." It does no good to ignore these ideas; they will inevitably crop up during the collaborative process. The better each agency understands the other, the less frustration each will experience.

Once everyone involved has a basic understanding of the goals and needs of the other agency, effective communication is possible. Clear communication includes defining the problem, articulating a common mission, and setting realistic goals.

Defining the Problem

Child welfare agencies and housing agencies together can identify the problems that they hope to resolve with closer collaboration. These are typical of problems that have been identified in communities around the country:

- In Contra Costa County, California, children are unable to return home from foster care primarily because their parents lack adequate housing, and children are placed into foster care for similar reasons.

- In St. Louis, families participating in a family preservation program need housing assistance to move away from violent partners and/or drug dealers.

- In Atlanta, families involved with the child welfare system are evicted from public housing and risk having their children placed in care.

In communities eligible for the federal FUP, the child welfare agency prepares a report that details the problems facing its clients as a part of the application. This report should be written in conjunction with the housing agency to be sure it meets the application criteria.

Articulating a Common Mission

Articulating a common mission will help focus and guide collaborative efforts.

Examples of a common mission include:

- To reduce the number of children delayed in returning to their parents when housing is a primary problem by [a date agreed on by both agencies].

- To create an ongoing child welfare/housing collaboration to improve services to families who receive assistance from both systems.

Setting Realistic Goals

Collaborating partners should set realistic goals for their collaboration. The goals can be revisited and revised frequently, but they must be clear and achievable. Below are some examples of collaborative goals:

- To apply jointly for FUP funds (in eligible communities)

- To use FUP resources to house 50 families whose children are at risk of placement in out-of-home care

- To blend funds to create a state-funded housing assistance program that will assist in the reunification of 20 families in its first year

Making It Happen

The crucial difference between communities that have instituted these collaborative programs and those that have not is the presence of people committed to initiating these programs and seeing them to fruition. You can be that person in your community. This manual provides all the information and strategies you need to make these collaborative efforts effective for families in your community. The tools in this manual, especially the numerous appendices, are valuable resources to use as you design and implement housing services for child welfare families in your community.

The Child Welfare League of America is committed to supporting these efforts with information, advocacy, and training.

References

For more information about collaboration, see these publications, from which some of the ideas in this section have been borrowed:

Bruner, Charles. (1991). *Thinking collaboratively: Ten questions and answers to help policy makers improve children's services.* Washington, DC: Education and Human Services Consortium.

Winer, M., & Ray, K. (1994). *Collaboration handbook: Creating, sustaining and enjoying the journey.* St. Paul, MN: Amherst Wilder Foundation.

Appendixes

Appendix A

Program Contacts and Consulting

This manual should serve as an resource for service providers and advocates in communities across the country. CWLA is available to help your community use this manual and other local techniques to establish and/or improve housing and support programs for families. Requests for technical assistance from CWLA should be directed to:

Yvonne A. Doerre or Bob McKay
  Child Welfare League of America
  440 First St., NW, Suite 310
  Washington, DC 20001
  202/638–2952
  Fax: 202/638–4004
  E-mail: ydoerre@cwla.org

Communities seeking assistance in developing medical services through FQHC and other avenues should contact:

Allan Katz
  Health Care Consultant
  7925 Winthrope St.
  Oakland, CA 94605
  510/569–8764
  Fax: 510/569–8458

Questions about specific HUD regulations cited in this manual should be directed to:

Gerald Benoit
  Director, Operations Branch
  Division of Public and Indian Housing
  U.S. Department of Housing and Urban
  Development
  Room 4220
  451 Seventh St. SW
  Washington, DC 20410
  202/708–0477
  E-mail: geraldj.benoit@hud.gov

Site Contacts

Questions about the practices described at specific sites are best addressed by the people implementing these practices at the local level.

Each of the activities in the text indicated with a ❤ is represented by a contact person listed below. Each of these contacts has agreed to be listed here and is willing to take calls and inquiries about their specific practices.

The contacts are listed in alphabetical order by state.

Arizona

Lauri Devine
Reasonable Efforts Specialist, Housing Assistance Program Arizona Department of Economic Security Division of Children and Family Services Administration for Children, Youth & Families
1789 W. Jefferson, Site Code 940 A
P.O. Box 6123
Phoenix, AZ 85005
602/542–5017

California—Contra Costa County

Mary Foran
Health Services Department
County of Costra County
20 Allen Street
Martinez, CA 94553
510/370–5010

California—Orange County

Louise Kaderlan
Orange County Dept. of Social Services
800 N. Eckhoff St.
Orange, CA 92668–1032
714/704–8857

California—San Jose

William Drennan
Family Preservation Program Specialist
Social Services Agency
Department of Children & Family Services
County of Santa Clara
1725 Technology Drive
San Jose, CA 95110
408/441–5275

Sandi Douglas
Community Services Manager
Housing Authority of the County of Santa Clara
505 W. Julian St.
San Jose, CA 95110
408/298–4103

Georgia—Atlanta

Fred Zachery
Human Resources Coordinator
Department of Children & Family Services
501 Pullian St. NW, Suite 525
Atlanta, GA 30312
404/657–6720

Illinois

John Cheney Egan
Housing Specialist
Office of Litigation Management
Illinois Department of Children & Families
160 N. LaSalle, 6th Fl.
Chicago, IL 60601–3105
312/814–1878

Maryland—Baltimore County

Maureen Robinson
Baltimore County Department of Social Services
One Investment Place
Towson, MD 21204
410/887–5551

Marilyn Ebaugh
Baltimore County Department of Community Development & Housing
One Investment Place
Towson, MD 21204
410/887–4000, x 49

Maryland—Montgomery County

Lillian Durham
  Assistant Director, Resident Services
  Director Housing Opportunities
  Commission of Montgomery County
  10400 Detrick Avenue
  Kensington, MD 20895-2484
  301/527-0034, x. 200

Agnes Farkas Leshner
  Chief, Child Welfare Services
  Department of Social Services
  401 Hungerford Drive
  Rockville, MD 20850
  301/217-3542

Massachusetts

Maryann Morrison   617/727-0532
Jennie Rawski   617/727-7130, x640
  Massachusetts Department of Economic
  Development, Division of Housing and
  Community Development
  100 Cambridge Street
  Boston, MA 02202

Paula Callahan
  Family Unification Program Coordinator
  Massachusetts Department of Social
  Services
  24 Farnsworth St.
  Boston, MA 02210
  617/727-3171, x554
  Fax: 617/727-3171

Missouri—St. Louis

Laurie Johnson
  (information on assessment tools)
  Citizens for Missouri's Children
  2717 Sutton Ave.
  St. Louis, MO 63143
  314/647-2003

Deborah Paulsrud
  (supervisor of student interns)
  George Warren Brown School of Social
  Work
  Washington University
  Campus Box 1196
  One Brookings Drive
  St. Louis, MO 63130-4899
  314/935-6678

Candace Iveson
  (multiagency committee, training
  conferences)
  Legal Services of Eastern Missouri
  4232 Forest Park Blvd.
  St. Louis, MO 63108
  314/534-4200, x1247

Missouri—Statewide

Carol Bisch
  (state legislation, Crisis Intervention
  Fund)
  Missouri Dept. of Social Services
  Division of Family Services, St. Louis City
  111 North 7th St.,
  Wainwright Bldg.
  St. Louis, MO 63101
  314/340-7042

New Jersey

Nancy Caplan
  (general contact, health services)
  Office of Placement and Permanency
  Services Division of Youth & Family
  Services
  50 East State Street/CN-717
  Trenton, NJ 08625-0717
  609/292-0887

Roy Ziegler
  (FUP and FSS information)
  New Jersey Department of Community
  Affairs
  Division of Housing and Community
  Resources
  101 South Broad Street
  Trenton, NJ 08625
  609/633-6150

New York—Ithaca

Marcy Hudson
  FSS & FUP Coordinator
  Ithaca Housing Authority
  800 South Plain Street
  Ithaca, NY 14850
  607/273-1244

New York—Statewide

Hal Harkess
  New York State Department of Social
  Services
  Division of Services & Community
  Development
  40 N. Pearl St., Section 11-D
  Albany, NY 12243
  518/474-9584

Family Unification Program Advisory Committee

Gerald Benoit
Director, Operations Branch
Division of Public and Indian Housing
U.S. Department of Housing and Urban
Development
Room 4220
451 Seventh St. SW
Washington, DC 20410
202/708–0477
E-mail: geraldj.benoit@hud.gov

Paula Callahan
Family Unification Program Coordinator
Massachusetts Department of Social
Services
24 Farnsworth St.
Boston, MA 02210
617/727–3171, x.554
Fax: 617/727–3171

John Cheney Egan
Housing Specialist
Office of Litigation Management
Illinois Department of Children &
Families
160 N. LaSalle, 6th Fl.
Chicago, IL 60601–3105
312/814–1878

Louise Kaderlan
Orange County Dept. of Social Services
800 N. Eckhoff St.
Orange, CA 92668-1032
714-704-8857
Fax: 714/541–7811

Dan Manning
Director of Litigation
Boston Legal Assistance Project
197 Friend Street
Boston, MA 02114
617/371–1234
Fax: 617/371–1222

Mary Ann Morrison
Director of Section 8
Massachusetts Department of Economic
Development, Division of Housing and
Community Development
100 Cambridge Street
Boston, MA 02202
617/727–0532

Bill Murphy
Housing Specialist
Office of Public and Assisted Housing
U.S. Dept. of Housing and Urban
Development
451 Seventh Street, SW
Washington, DC 20410
202/708–0477
Fax: 202/401–6867

Deborah Paulsrud
GWB School of Social Work
Washington University
One Brookings Drive
Campus Box 1196
St. Louis, MO 63130
314/935–6678
Fax: 314/935–8511

Steve Renahan
Section 8 Director
Los Angeles Housing Authority
2650 Wilshire Boulevard, Rm. 5600
Los Angeles, CA 90057
213/252–2570
Fax: 213/252–2650

Maureen Robinson
    Housing Coordinator
    Dept. of Social Services
    Baltimore County DSS
    One Investment Place
    Towson, MD 21204
    410/887–5551
    Fax: 410/887–5820

Debra Rog
    Director
    Institute for Public Policy Research
    Vanderbilt University, Suite 401
    1609 Connecticut Avenue, NW
    Washington, DC 20009
    202/234–1190
    Fax: 202/234–1185

Cecilia Sudia
    Family Services Specialist
    Children's Bureau
    P.O. Box 1182
    Washington, DC 20201
    202/205–8764
    Fax: 202/401–5917

Ray Worsham
    Program Specialist
    Texas Dept. of Protective & Regulatory
    Services
    P.O. Box 149030
    Austin, TX 78714
    512/450–3362
    Fax: 512/459–3782

Roy Ziegler
    Assistant Director
    New Jersey Department of Community
    Affairs
    Division of Housing and Community
    Resources
    101 South Broad Street
    Trenton, NJ 08625
    609/633–6150
    Fax: 609/633–8084

Appendix B

Amended Administration Plan Establishing a Ranking Preference: Massachusetts

EXECUTIVE
OFFICE OF
COMMUNITIES &
DEVELOPMENT

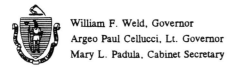

William F. Weld, Governor
Argeo Paul Cellucci, Lt. Governor
Mary L. Padula, Cabinet Secretary

September 22, 1994

Ms. Doris Desautel
Director
Office of Public and Indian Housing
U.S. Department of Housing and Urban Development
10 Causeway Street
Boston, MA. 02202-1092

Attention: Mr. Stanley Sigel

RE: EOCD Request to Amend Its Section 8 Tenant Selection
           Criteria

Dear Ms. Desautel:

     The Massachusetts Executive Office of Communities and
Development (EOCD) requests HUD permission to amend its current
Section 8 tenant selection criteria in order to include an
additional first preference category as follows:

> First preference shall also be provided to applicants who
> qualify for EOCD's Family Unification Program pilot
> program.

> This preference will be provided to no more than seventy-
> five voucher recipients. Recipients wishing to switch
> from a voucher to a certificate may do so in accordance
> with HUD requirements and established EOCD procedures.

     On several occasions, we have been advised by HUD Central
office staff that HUD encourages PHAs to use their conventional
Section 8 portfolio to expand special initiatives, like the Family
Unification Program. Further, we believe that this request is
consistent with a PHA's ability to use a local preference criteria
to select from among federal preference holders.

     Our current family unification pilot program is quite
successful and the Massachusetts Department of Social Services
(DSS), the Commonwealth's child welfare agency, has requested that
we explore the possibility of expanding it.

100 Cambridge Street
Boston, Massachusetts 02202

We are proposing to use increased voucher contract authority to subsidize the expansion of this initiative.

I am including for your review a copy of our current HUD approved Family Unification Program administrative guidelines. We will continue to utilize these criteria when the program is expanded with the seventy-five vouchers.

Thank-you for your prompt attention to this request.

Sincerely,

Mary-Anne Morrison
Director
Bureau of Federal Rental Assistance

fup2.hud

Appendix C

U.S. Department of Housing and Urban Development Family Unification Program, FY 1996 NOFA

Thursday
May 2, 1996

Part V

Department of Housing and Urban Development

Notice of Funding Availability for the Family Unification Program, Fiscal Year 1996; Notice

DEPARTMENT OF HOUSING AND URBAN DEVELOPMENT

[Docket No. FR–4045–N–01]

Office of the Assistant Secretary for Public and Indian Housing; NOFA for the Family Unification Program, Fiscal Year 1996

AGENCY: Office of the Assistant Secretary for Public and Indian Housing, HUD.

ACTION: Notice of funding availability (NOFA) for FY 1996.

SUMMARY: This notice announces the availability of up to $32 million (approximately) in 2-year budget authority for FY 1996 for section 8 rental certificates under the Family Unification Program, which will support approximately 1,600 families. Public housing agencies (PHAs) and Indian Housing Authorities (IHAs), herein referred to as housing agencies (HAs), are invited to submit applications for housing assistance.

The purpose of the Family Unification Program is to provide housing assistance to families for whom the lack of adequate housing is a primary factor in the separation, or imminent separation, of children from their families. As was the case in prior years, participation in the Family Unification Program is limited to HAs in 16 States. The 16 States are: California, Florida, Georgia, Illinois, Maryland, Massachusetts, Michigan, Minnesota, Missouri, New Jersey, New York, North Carolina, Ohio, Pennsylvania, Texas, and Virginia.

DATES: The application deadline for the Family Unification program NOFA is July 1, 1996, 3:00 p.m., local time.

The above-stated application deadline is firm as to date and hour. In the interest of fairness to all competing HAs, HUD will treat as ineligible for consideration any application that is not received before the application deadline. Applicants should take this practice into account and make early submission of their materials to avoid any risk of loss of eligibility brought about by unanticipated delays or other delivery-related problems. HUD will not accept, at any time during the NOFA competition, application materials sent via facsimile (FAX) transmission.

ADDRESSES: The local HUD State or Area Office, Attention: Director, Office of Public Housing, is the official place of receipt for all applications, except applications from Indian Housing Authorities (IHAs). The local HUD Native American Programs Office, Attention: Administrator, Office of Native American Programs, is the place of official receipt for IHA applications. For ease of reference, the term "HUD Office" will be used throughout this NOFA to mean the HUD State Office, HUD Area Office, and the HUD Native American Programs Office. If a particular type of HUD Office needs to be identified, e.g., the HUD Native American Programs Office, the appropriate office will be used.

FOR FURTHER INFORMATION CONTACT: Gerald J. Benoit, Director, Operations Division, Office of Rental Assistance, Department of Housing and Urban Development, 451 Seventh Street, SW., Washington, DC 20410–8000, telephone number (202) 708–0477 (this is not a toll-free number). For hearing- and speech-impaired persons, this number may be accessed via TTY (text telephone) by calling the Federal Information Relay Service at 1–800–877–8339.

SUPPLEMENTARY INFORMATION:

Paperwork Reduction Act Statement

The section 8 information collection requirements contained in this NOFA have been approved by the Office of Management and Budget in accordance with the Paperwork Reduction Act of 1995 (44 U.S.C. 3501–3520), and assigned OMB control number 2577–0169. An agency may not conduct or sponsor, and a person is not required to respond to, a collection of information unless the collection displays a valid control number.

Family Self-Sufficiency (FSS) Program Requirement

Unless specifically exempted by HUD, all rental voucher or rental certificate funding reserved in FY 1996 (except funding for renewals or amendments) will be used to establish the minimum size of an HA's FSS program.

A. Purpose and Substantive Description of Family Unification Program

(1) Authority. The Family Unification Program is authorized by Section 8(x) of the United States Housing Act of 1937, 42 U.S.C. 1437f(x).

(2) Background. The Family Unification Program is a program under which Section 8 rental assistance is provided to families for whom the lack of adequate housing is a primary factor which would result in:

(a) The imminent placement of the family's child, or children, in out-of-home care; or

(b) The delay in the discharge of the child, or children, to the family from out-of-home care.

The purpose of the Family Unification Program is to promote family unification by providing rental assistance to families for whom the lack of adequate housing is a primary factor in the separation, or the threat of imminent separation, of children from their families.

Rental certificates awarded under the Family Unification Program are to be administered by HAs under HUD's regulations for the Section 8 rental certificate program (24 CFR parts 882 and 982). The HA may issue a rental voucher (24 CFR parts 887 and 982) to a family selected for participation in the Family Unification Program if the family requests a rental voucher and the HA has one available.

(3) Eligibility of HAs.—(a) Family Unification Program Eligibility. Consistent with previous NOFAs, HAs currently administering a rental voucher or certificate program in the following 16 States are eligible to apply (except those HAs determined unacceptable under section A.(3)(b) of this NOFA): California, Florida, Georgia, Illinois, Maryland, Massachusetts, Michigan, Minnesota, Missouri, New Jersey, New York, North Carolina, Ohio, Pennsylvania, Texas, and Virginia.

(b) *Eligibility for HUD-Designated Housing Agencies with Major Program Findings.* HUD will establish a pass or fail threshold for all HAs. An HA that fails the threshold will not be eligible to apply without another entity to administer the program. Some housing agencies currently administering the Section 8 rental voucher and certificate programs have, at the time of publication of this NOFA, major program management findings that are open and unresolved or other significant program compliance problems (e.g., HA has not implemented mandatory FSS program). HUD will not accept applications for additional funding from these HAs as contract administrators if, on the application deadline date, the findings are not closed to HUD's satisfaction. If these HAs want to apply for the Family Unification Program, the HA must submit an application that designates another housing agency, nonprofit agency, or contractor that is acceptable to HUD and includes an agreement with the other housing agency or contractor to administer the new funding increment on behalf of the HA. The Office of Public Housing in the local HUD Office will notify, immediately after the publication of this NOFA, those HAs that are not eligible to apply. Applications submitted by these HAs without an agreement from another housing agency or contractor, approved by HUD, to serve as contract administrator will be rejected. Other agencies may be notified by HUD at other times as HUD deems appropriate.

(4) Program Guidelines.—(a) *Eligibility.*—(i) *Family Unification eligible families.* Each HA must modify, in accordance with program rules, its selection preference system to permit the selection of Family Unification eligible families for the program based on available funding provided by HUD for this purpose. The term "Family Unification eligible family" means a family that:

(A) The public child welfare agency has certified is a family for whom the lack of adequate housing is a primary factor in the imminent placement of the family's child, or children, in out-of-home care, or in the delay of discharge of a child, or children, to the family from out-of-home care; and

(B) The HA has determined is eligible for Section 8 rental assistance.

(ii) *Lack of Adequate Housing.* The lack of adequate housing means:

(A) A family is living in substandard housing; or

(B) A family is homeless; or

(C) A family is displaced by domestic violence; or

(D) A family is living in an overcrowded unit.

(iii) *Substandard Housing.* A family is living in substandard housing if the unit where the family lives:

(A) Is dilapidated;

(B) Does not have operable indoor plumbing;

(C) Does not have a usable flush toilet inside the unit for the exclusive use of a family;

(D) Does not have a usable bathtub or shower inside the unit for the exclusive use of a family;

(E) Does not have electricity, or has inadequate or unsafe electrical service;

(F) Does not have a safe or adequate source of heat;

(G) Should, but does not, have a kitchen; or

(H) Has been declared unfit for habitation by an agency or unit or government.

(iv) *Dilapidated Housing.* A family is living in a housing unit that is dilapidated if it does not provide safe and adequate shelter, and in its present condition endangers the health, safety, or well-being of a family, or it has one or more critical defects, or a combination of intermediate defects in sufficient number or extent to require considerable repair or rebuilding. The defects may involve original construction, or they may result from continued neglect or lack of repair or from serious damage to the structure.

(v) *Homeless.* A homeless family includes any person or family that:

(A) Lacks a fixed, regular, and adequate nighttime residence; and

(B) Has a primary nighttime residence that is:

(1) A supervised publicly or privately operated shelter designed to provide temporary living accommodations (including welfare hotels, congregate shelters, and transitional housing);

(2) An institution that provides a temporary residence for persons intended to be institutionalized; or

(3) A public or private place not designed for, or ordinarily used as, a regular sleeping accommodation for human beings.

(vi) *Detained Family.* A Family Unification eligible family does not include any person imprisoned or otherwise detained pursuant to an Act of the Congress or a State law.

(vii) *Displaced by Domestic Violence.* A family is displaced by domestic violence if:

(A) The applicant has vacated a housing unit because of domestic violence; or

(B) The applicant lives in a housing unit with a person who engages in domestic violence.

(C) "Domestic violence" means actual or threatened physical violence directed against one or more members of the applicant family by a spouse or other member of the applicant's household.

(viii) *Qualify as Involuntarily Displaced.* For an applicant to qualify as involuntarily displaced because of domestic violence:

(A) The HA must determine that the domestic violence occurred recently or is of a continuing nature; and

(B) The applicant must certify that the person who engaged in such violence will not reside with the applicant family unless the HA has given advance written approval. If the family is admitted, the HA may deny or terminate assistance to the family for breach of this certification.

(ix) *Overcrowded Housing.* A family is considered to be living in an overcrowded unit if:

(A) The family is separated from its children and the parent(s) are living in an otherwise standard housing unit, but, after the family is re-united, the parents' housing unit would be overcrowded for the entire family and would be considered substandard.

(B) The family is living with its children in a unit that is overcrowded for the entire family and this overcrowded condition may result in the imminent placement of a child or children in out-of-home care.

(C) For purpose of this paragraph (ix), the HA shall have discretion to determine whether the unit is

"overcrowded" in accordance with HA occupancy standards.

(x) *Public child welfare agency* (PCWA) means the public agency that is responsible under applicable State or Tribal law for determining that a child is at imminent risk of placement in out-of-home care or that a child in out-of-home care under the supervision of the public agency may be returned to his or her family.

(b) *HA Responsibilities.* HAs must:

(i) Accept families certified by the PCWA as eligible for the Family Unification Program. If the HA has a closed waiting list, it must reopen the waiting list to accept Family Unification Program applicant families. The HA is not required to review its waiting list for eligible families. The HA upon receipt of the PCWA list of families currently in the PCWA caseload must compare the names with those of families already on the HA's Section 8 waiting list. Any family on the HA's Section 8 waiting list that matches with the PCWA's list must be assisted in order of their position on the waiting list in accordance with HA admission policies;

(ii) Determine if any families with children on its waiting list are living in temporary shelters or on the street and may qualify for the Family Unification Program, and refer such applicants to the PCWA;

(iii) Determine if families referred by the PCWA are eligible for Section 8 assistance and place eligible families on the Section 8 waiting list;

(iv) Amend the administrative plan in accordance with applicable program regulations and requirements;

(v) Administer the rental assistance in accordance with applicable program regulations and requirements; and

(vi) Assure the quality of the evaluation that HUD intends to conduct on the Family Unification Program and cooperate with and provide requested data to the HUD office or HUD-approved contractor responsible for program evaluation.

(c) *Public Child Welfare Agency (PCWA) Responsibilities.* Public child welfare agencies must:

(i) Establish and implement a system to identify Family Unification eligible families within the agency's caseload and to review referrals from the HA;

(ii) Provide written certification to the HA that a family qualifies as a Family Unification eligible family based upon the criteria established in Section 8(x) of the United States Housing Act of 1937, HUD regulations, and the HA policies implementing the regulations;

(iii) Commit sufficient staff resources to ensure that Family Unification eligible families are identified and certified in a timely manner and to provide follow-up supportive services after the families lease units; and

(iv) Cooperate with the evaluation that HUD intends to conduct on the Family Unification Program, and submit a certification with the HA's application for Family Unification funding that the PCWA will agree to cooperate with and provide requested data to the HUD office or HUD-approved contractor having responsibility for program evaluation.

(d) *Section 8 Rental Certificate Assistance.* The Family Unification Program provides assistance under the Section 8 rental assistance programs. Although HUD is providing a special allocation of rental certificates, the HA may use both rental vouchers and certificates to assist families under this program.

HAs must administer this program in accordance with HUD's regulations governing the Section 8 rental certificate and rental voucher programs. The HA may issue a rental voucher to a family selected to participate in the Family Unification Program if the family requests a rental voucher and the HA has one available. If Section 8 assistance for a family under this program is terminated, the rental assistance must be reissued to another Family Unification eligible family during the 2-year term of the Annual Contributions Contract (ACC) for the Section 8 rental certificates provided under this program.

B. Family Unification Allocation Amounts

This NOFA announces the availability of up to $32 million for the Family Unification Program which will support assistance for about 1,600 families. Each HA may apply for funding for a maximum of 50 units.

The amounts allocated under this NOFA will be awarded under a national competition, based on the threshold criteria and a lottery for selection from all approvable applications. The Family Unification Program is exempt from the fair share allocation requirements of section 213(d) of the Housing and Community Development Act of 1974 (42 U.S.C. 1439(d)) and the implementing regulations at 24 CFR part 791, subpart D. Applications that meet the requirements of this NOFA and are included in the FY 1996 lottery, but that are not selected, may be considered for funding from funds available, if any, in FY 1997 appropriations designated for the Family Unification Program.

C. Family Unification Application Submission Requirements

(1) Forms. Application forms may be obtained from the local HUD Office. Applications must include the following, unless otherwise specifically excepted:

(a) *Form HUD–52515.* An Application for Existing Housing, Form HUD–52515, must be completed in accordance with the program regulations (24 CFR 982.102). An application must include the information in Section C, Average Monthly Adjusted Income, of Form HUD–52515 in order for HUD to calculate the amount of Section 8 budget authority necessary to fund the requested number of units. HAs may obtain a copy of Form HUD–52515 from the local HUD Office.

(b) *Certification Regarding Drug-Free Workplace.* The Drug-Free Workplace Act of 1988 requires grantees of Federal agencies to certify that they will provide a drug-free workplace. Thus, each HA must certify (even though it has done so previously) that it will comply with the drug-free workplace requirements in accordance with CFR part 24, subpart F. HAs may obtain a copy of this form from the local HUD Office.

(c) *Certification Regarding Lobbying.* Any HA submitting an application under this announcement for more than $100,000 of budget authority must submit a certification and, if applicable, a Disclosure of Lobbying Activities (SF–LLL). IHAs established by an Indian tribe as a result of the exercise of the tribe's sovereign power are excluded from coverage, but IHAs established under State law are not excluded from the coverage. HAs may obtain a copy of the certification and the Form SF–LLL from the local HUD Office.

(2) Local government comments. Section 213 of the Housing and Community Development Act of 1974 requires that HUD independently determine that there is a need for the housing assistance requested in applications and solicit and consider comments relevant to this determination from the chief executive officer of the unit of general local government. The HUD Office will obtain Section 213 comments from the unit of general local government in accordance with 24 CFR part 791, subpart C, Applications for Housing Assistance in Areas Without Housing Assistance Plans. Comments submitted by the unit of general local government must be considered before an application can be approved.

For purposes of expediting the application process, the HA should encourage the chief executive officer of the unit of general local government to submit a letter with the HA application commenting on the HA application in accordance with Section 213. Because HUD cannot approve an application until the 30-day comment period is closed, the Section 213 letter should not only comment on the application, but also state that HUD may consider the letter to be the final comments and that no additional comments will be forthcoming from the unit of general local government.

(3) Letter of Intent and Narrative. All the items in this Section must be included in the application submitted to the HUD Office. The HA must state in its cover letter to the application whether it will accept a reduction in the number of rental certificates and the minimum number of rental certificates it will accept, since the funding is limited and HUD may only have enough funds to approve a smaller amount than the number of rental certificates requested. The application must include an explanation of how the application meets, or will meet, Threshold Criteria 1 through 4 in Section D of this NOFA, below.

The application must also include a letter of intent from the PCWA stating its commitment to provide resources and support for the Family Unification Program. The PCWA letter of intent must explain:

(i) The definition of eligible families;
(ii) The method used to identify eligible families;
(iii) The process to certify eligible families;
(iv) The PCWA assistance to families to locate suitable housing;
(v) The staff resources committed to the program; and
(vi) PCWA experience with the administration of similar programs including cooperation with a HA.

The PCWA serving the jurisdiction of the HA is responsible for providing the information for Threshold Criterion 4, PCWA Statement of Need for Family Unification Program, to the HA for submission with the HA application. The application must include a statement by the PCWA describing the need for a Family Unification Program. This should include a discussion of the case-load of the PCWA and information about homelessness, family violence resulting in involuntary displacement, number and characteristics of families who are experiencing the placement of children in out-of-home care as a result of inadequate housing, and the PCWA's experience in obtaining housing through HUD assisted housing programs and other sources for families lacking adequate housing. A State-wide Public Child Welfare Agency must provide information on Threshold Criterion 4, PCWA Statement of Need for Family Unification Program, to all HAs that request data; otherwise, HUD will not consider applications from any HAs with the State-wide PCWA as a participant in its program.

(4) Evaluation Certifications. The HA and the PCWA, in separate certifications, must state that the HA and Public Child Welfare Agency agree to cooperate with HUD and provide requested data to the HUD office or HUD-approved contractor delegated the responsibility for the program evaluation. No specific language for this certification is prescribed by HUD.

D. Family Unification Application Rating Process

(1) General. The HUD Office is responsible for rating the applications for the selection criteria established in this NOFA, and HUD Headquarters is responsible for selection of applications (including applications rated by the Native American Programs Office) that will receive assistance under the Family Unification Program. The HUD Office will initially screen all applications and determine any technical deficiencies based on the application submission requirements.

Each application submitted in response to the NOFA, in order to be eligible for funding, must receive at least 30 points for Threshold Criterion 1, Unmet Housing Needs, and at least 20 points for Threshold Criterion 2, Efforts of HA to Provide Area-Wide Housing Opportunities for Families, and must meet the requirements for Threshold Criterion 3, Coordination between HA and Public Child Welfare Agency, and Threshold Criterion 4, Public Child Welfare Agency Statement of Need for Family Unification Program.

(2) Threshold Criteria.
(a) *THRESHOLD CRITERION 1: UNMET HOUSING NEEDS (50 POINTS).*

(i) *Description:* This criterion assesses the unmet housing need in the primary area specified in the HA's application compared to the unmet housing need for the allocation area. Unmet housing need is defined as the number of very low-income renter households with housing problems based on 1990 Census, minus the number of federally assisted housing units provided since the 1990 Census.

In awarding points under this criterion, HUD will, to the extent practicable, consider all units provided since the 1990 Census under the Section 8 Rental Voucher and Certificate programs, any other Section 8 programs, the Public and Indian Housing programs, the Section 202 program, and the Farmers Home Administration's Section 515 Rural Rental Housing program.

(ii) *Rating and Assessment:* The number of points assigned is based on the percentage of the allocation area's unmet housing need that is within the HA's primary area. State or Regional Housing Agencies will receive points based on the areas they intend to serve with this allocation, e.g., the entire allocation area or the localities within the allocation area specified in the application. The HUD Office will assign one of the following point totals:

• *50 points.* If the HA's percentage of unmet housing need is greater than 50 percent of the allocation area's unmet need.

• *45 points.* If the HA's percentage of unmet housing need is equal to or less than 50 percent but greater than 40 percent of the allocation area's unmet need.

• *40 points.* If the HA's percentage of unmet housing need is equal to or less than 40 percent but greater than 30 percent of the allocation area's unmet need.

• *35 points.* If the HA's percentage of unmet housing need is equal to or less than 30 percent but greater than 20 percent of the allocation area's unmet need.

• *30 points.* If the HA's percentage of unmet housing need is equal to or less than 20 percent but greater than 10 percent of the allocation area's unmet need.

• *0 points.* If the HA's percentage of unmet housing need is equal to or less than 10 percent of the allocation area's unmet need.

The HUD Office will not consider for funding any HA application receiving zero (0) points.

In accordance with Notice PIH 91–45, the HUD Office will notify the Farmers Home Administration, or its successor agency under Public Law 103–354 (FmHA), of applications it receives and ask that FmHA provide advisory comments concerning the market for additional assisted housing or the possible impact the proposed units may have on FmHA projects. Applications for which FmHA has provided comments expressing concerns about market need or the continued stability of existing FmHA projects, with which HUD agrees, will receive zero points for this criterion.

(b) *THRESHOLD CRITERION 2: EFFORTS OF HA TO PROVIDE AREA-WIDE HOUSING OPPORTUNITIES FOR FAMILIES (60 POINTS).*

(i) *Description:* Many HAs have undertaken voluntary efforts to provide area-wide housing opportunities for families. The efforts described in response to this selection criterion must be beyond those required by federal law or regulation such as the portability provisions of the Section 8 rental voucher and certificate programs. HAs in metropolitan and non-metropolitan areas are eligible for points under this criterion. The HUD Office will assign points to HAs that have established cooperative agreements with other HAs or created a consortium of HAs in order to facilitate the transfer of families and their rental assistance between HA jurisdictions. In addition, the HUD Office will assign points to HAs that have established relationships with nonprofit groups to provide families with additional counseling, or have directly provided counseling, to increase the likelihood of a successful move by the families to areas that do not have large concentrations of poverty.

(ii) *Rating and Assessment:* The HUD Office will assign point values for any of the following assessments for which the HA qualifies and add the points for all the assessments (maximum of 60 points) to determine the total points for this Selection Criterion:

• *10 points*—Assign 10 points if the HA documents that it participates in an area-wide rental voucher and certificate exchange program where all HAs absorb portable Section 8 families.

• *10 Points*—Assign 10 points if the HA certifies that its administrative plan does not include a "residency preference" for selection of families to participate in its rental voucher and certificate programs or the HA certifies that it will eliminate immediately any "residency preference" currently in its administrative plan.

• *10 Points*—Assign 10 points if the HA documents that it has established a contractual relationship with a nonprofit agency or the local governmental entity to provide housing counseling for families that want to move to low-poverty or non-minority areas. The five HAs approved for the FY 1993 Moving to Opportunity (MTO) for Fair Housing Demonstration and any other HAs that receive counseling funds from HUD (e.g., in settlement of litigation involving desegregation or demolition of public housing, mixed population projects) may qualify for points under this assessment, but these HAs must identify all activities undertaken, other than those funded by HUD, to expand housing opportunities.

• *10 Points*—Assign 10 points if the HA documents that it requested from HUD, and HUD approved, the authority to utilize exceptions to the fair market rent limitations as allowed under 24 CFR 882.106(a)(4) to allow families to select units in low-poverty or non-minority areas.

• *10 Points*—Assign 10 points if the HA documents that it participates with other HAs in using a metropolitan wide or combined waiting list for selecting participants in the program.

• *10 Points*—Assign 10 points if the HA documents that it has implemented other initiatives that have resulted in expanding housing opportunities in areas that do not have undue concentrations of poverty or minority families.

(c) *THRESHOLD CRITERION 3: COORDINATION BETWEEN HA AND PUBLIC CHILD WELFARE AGENCY TO IDENTIFY AND ASSIST ELIGIBLE FAMILIES.*

The application must describe the method that the HA and the PCWA will use to identify and assist Family Unification eligible families. The application must include a letter of intent from the PCWA stating its commitment to provide resources and support for the program. The PCWA letter of intent and other information must be comprehensive and must include an explanation of: the method used to identify eligible families, the PCWA's certification process for determining Family Unification eligible families, the responsibilities of each agency, the PCWA assistance provided to families in locating housing units, the PCWA staff resources committed to the program, the past PCWA experience administering a similar program, and the PCWA/HA cooperation in administering a similar program.

(d) *THRESHOLD CRITERION 4: PUBLIC CHILD WELFARE AGENCY STATEMENT OF NEED FOR FAMILY UNIFICATION PROGRAM.*

The application must include a statement by the PCWA describing the need for a program providing assistance to families for whom lack of adequate housing is a primary factor in the placement of the family's children in out-of-home care or in the delay of discharge of the children to the family from out-of-home care in the area to be served, as evidenced by the caseload of the public child welfare agency. The PCWA must adequately demonstrate that there is a need in the HA's jurisdiction for the Family Unification program that is not being met through existing programs. The narrative must include specific information relevant to the area to be served, about homelessness, family violence resulting in involuntary displacement, number and characteristics of families who are experiencing the placement of children in out-of-home care or the delayed discharge of children from out-of-home

care as the result of inadequate housing, and the PCWA's past experience in obtaining housing through HUD assisted programs and other sources for families lacking adequate housing.

E. Corrections to Deficient Family Unification Applications

(1) Acceptable Applications. To be eligible for processing, an application must be received by the appropriate HUD Office no later than the date and time specified in this NOFA. The HUD Office will initially screen all applications and notify HAs of technical deficiencies by letter.

If an application has technical deficiencies, the HA will have 14 calendar days from the date of the issuance of the HUD notification letter to submit the missing or corrected information to the HUD Office. Curable technical deficiencies relate only to items that do not improve the substantive quality of the application relative to the rating factors.

All HAs must submit corrections within 14 calendar days from the date of the HUD letter notifying the applicant of any such deficiency. Information received after 3 p.m. local time (i.e., the time in the appropriate HUD Office), of the 14th calendar day of the correction period will not be accepted and the application will be rejected as incomplete.

(2) Unacceptable Applications. (a) After the 14-calendar day technical deficiency correction period, the HUD Office will disapprove HA applications that it determines are not acceptable for processing. The HUD Office notification of rejection letter must state the basis for the decision.

(b) Applications that fall into any of the following categories will not be processed:

(i) There is a pending civil rights suit against the HA instituted by the Department of Justice or there is a pending administrative action for civil rights violations instituted by HUD (including a charge of discrimination under the Fair Housing Act).

(ii) There has been an adjudication of a civil rights violation in a civil action brought against the HA by a private individual, unless the HA is operating in compliance with a court order or implementing a HUD-approved resident selection and assignment plan or compliance agreement designed to correct the areas of noncompliance.

(iii) There are outstanding findings of noncompliance with civil rights statutes, Executive Orders, or regulations, as a result of formal administrative proceedings, or the Secretary has issued a charge against the

applicant under the Fair Housing Act, unless the applicant is operating under a conciliation or compliance agreement designed to correct the areas of noncompliance.

(iv) HUD has denied application processing under Title VI of the Civil Rights Act of 1964, the Attorney General's Guidelines (28 CFR 50.3), and the HUD Title VI regulations (24 CFR 1.8) and procedures (HUD Handbook 8040.1), or under section 504 of the Rehabilitation Act of 1973 and HUD regulations (24 CFR 8.57).

(v) The HA has serious unaddressed, outstanding Inspector General audit findings, Fair Housing and Equal Opportunity monitoring review findings, or HUD management review findings for one or more of its Rental Voucher, Rental Certificate, or Moderate Rehabilitation Programs, or, in the case of a HA that is not currently administering a Rental Voucher, Rental Certificate, or Moderate Rehabilitation Program, for its Public Housing Program or Indian Housing Program. The only exception to this category is if the HA has been identified under the policy established in section A.(3)(b) of this NOFA and the HA makes application with a designated contract administrator.

(vi) The HA is involved in litigation and HUD determines that the litigation may seriously impede the ability of the HA to administer an additional increment of rental vouchers or rental certificates.

(vii) A HA application that does not comply with the requirements of 24 CFR 982.102 and this NOFA, after the expiration of the 14-calendar day technical deficiency correction period will be rejected from processing.

(viii) A HA application submitted after the deadline date.

(ix) The application is from a HA that has failed to achieve a lease-up rate of 90 percent of units in its HUD-approved budget for the HA fiscal year prior to application for funding in each of its rental voucher and certificate programs.

F. Family Unification Application Selection Process

After the HUD Office has screened HA applications and disapproved any applications unacceptable for further processing (See Section E.(2) of this NOFA), the HUD Office will review and rate all approvable applications, utilizing the Threshold Criteria and the point assignments listed in this NOFA. Each HUD Office will send to HUD Headquarters the following information on each application that passes the Threshold Criteria:

(1) Name and address of the HA;

(2) Name and address of the Public Child Welfare Agency;

(3) State Office, Area Office, or Native American Programs Office contact person and telephone number;

(4) The number of rental certificates in the HA application and minimum number of rental certificates specified in the HA application, and the corresponding budget authority acceptable to the HA; and

(5) A completed fund reservation worksheet for the number of rental certificates requested in the application.

HUD Headquarters will select eligible HAs to be funded based on a lottery. All HAs identified by the HUD Offices as meeting the Threshold Criteria identified in this NOFA will be eligible for the lottery selection process. As HAs are selected, the costs of funding the applications will be counted against the total funds available for the Family Unification Program. In order to achieve geographic diversity, HUD Headquarters will limit the number of applications selected for funding under the lottery for any State to 10 percent of the budget authority made available under this NOFA.

Applications will be funded in full for the number of rental certificates requested by the HA in accordance with the NOFA. However, when remaining rental certificate funds are insufficient to fund the last HA application in full, HUD Headquarters may fund that application to the extent of the funding available and the applicant's willingness to accept a reduced number of rental certificates. Applicants that do not wish to have the size of their programs reduced may indicate in their applications that they do not wish to be considered for a reduced award of funds. HUD Headquarters will skip over these applicants if assigning the remaining funding would result in a reduced funding level.

G. Other Matters

Environmental Impact

A Finding of No Significant Impact with respect to the environment for all funding available under this NOFA has been made in accordance with the Department's regulations at 24 CFR part 50, which implement section 102(2)(C) of the National Environmental Policy Act of 1969 (42 U.S.C. 4332). The Finding is available for public inspection between 7:30 a.m. and 5:30 p.m. weekdays in the Office of the Rules Docket Clerk, Office of General Counsel, Department of Housing and Urban Development, room 10276, 451 Seventh Street, SW, Washington, D.C. 20410.

Federalism Impact

The General Counsel, as the Designated Official under section 6(a) of Executive Order 12612, *Federalism,* has determined that the policies contained in this notice will not have substantial direct effects on States or their political subdivisions, or the relationship between the Federal Government and the States, or on the distribution of power and responsibilities among the various levels of government. As a result, the notice is not subject to review under the Order. This notice is a funding notice and does not substantially alter the established roles of the Department, the States, and local governments, including HAs.

Impact on the Family

The General Counsel, as the Designated Official under Executive Order 12606, *The Family,* has determined that this notice does not have potential for significant impact on family formation, maintenance, and general well-being within the meaning of the Executive Order and, thus, is not subject to review under the Order. This is a funding notice and does not alter program requirements concerning family eligibility.

Section 102 of the HUD Reform Act: Documentation and Public Access Requirements

HUD will ensure that documentation and other information regarding each application submitted pursuant to this NOFA are sufficient to indicate the basis upon which assistance was provided or denied. This material, including any letters of support, will be made available for public inspection for a five-year period beginning not less than 30 calendar days after the award of the assistance. Material will be made available in accordance with the Freedom of Information Act (5 U.S.C. 552) and HUD's implementing regulations at 24 CFR part 15. In addition, HUD will include the recipients of assistance pursuant to this NOFA in its **Federal Register** notice of all recipients of HUD assistance awarded on a competitive basis. (See 24 CFR 12.14(a) and 12.16(b), and the notice published in the **Federal Register** on January 16, 1992 (57 FR 1942), for further information on these requirements.)

Section 103 of the HUD Reform Act

HUD's regulation implementing section 103 of the Department of Housing and Urban Development Reform Act of 1989 (42 U.S.C. 3537a) (Reform Act), codified as 24 CFR part 4, applies to the funding competition

announced today. The requirements of the rule continue to apply until the announcement of the selection of successful applicants.

HUD employees involved in the review of applications and in the making of funding decisions are restrained by part 4 from providing advance information to any person (other than an authorized employee of HUD) concerning funding decisions, or from otherwise giving any applicant an unfair competitive advantage. Persons who apply for assistance in this competition should confine their inquiries to the subject areas permitted under 24 CFR part 4.

Applicants or employees who have ethics-related questions should contact the HUD Office of Ethics (202) 708–3815 (TDD/Voice) (this is not a toll-free number). Any HUD employee who has specific program questions, such as whether particular subject matter can be discussed with persons outside the Department, should contact the appropriate Field Office Counsel or Headquarters counsel for the program to which the question pertains.

Prohibition Against Lobbying Activities

The use of funds awarded under this NOFA is subject to the disclosure requirements and prohibitions of section 319 of the Department of Interior and Related Agencies Appropriations Act for Fiscal Year 1990 (31 U.S.C. 1352) (the "Byrd Amendment") and the implementing regulations at 24 CFR part 87. These authorities prohibit recipients of Federal contracts, grants, or loans from using appropriated funds for lobbying the Executive or Legislative Branches of the Federal Government in connection with specific contract, grant, or loan. The prohibition also covers the awarding of contracts, grants, cooperative agreements, or loans unless the recipient has made an acceptable certification regarding lobbying. Under 24 CFR part 87, applicants, recipients, and subrecipients of assistance exceeding $100,000 must certify that no Federal funds have been or will be spent on lobbying activities in connection with the assistance. IHAs established by an Indian tribe as a result of the exercise of the tribe's sovereign power are excluded from coverage of the Byrd Amendment, but IHAs established under State law are not excluded from the statute's coverage.

Dated: April 23, 1996.

Michael B. Janis,

General Deputy Assistant Secretary for Public and Indian Housing.

[FR Doc. 96–10886 Filed 5–1–96; 8:45 am]

BILLING CODE 4210–33–P

Appendix D

CWLA's FY 1992 FUP Survey and Results

Family Unification Program 1st Year Grantees Child Welfare Agency Information Survey

Agency ______________________________

# of Units ______________________________

1. Please categorize your agency's general experience with the Family Unification Program.

Excellent Good Fair Poor Very Poor

1 2 3 4 5 6 7

2. Did you carry primary responsibility for the program?

____

3. Do you supervise caseworkers or do you carry your own caseload of families?

____

Were you able to refer families for the FUP without consulting a supervisor?

____

4. How were families identified for the program?

_____ all caseworkers reviewed files   _____ accepted referrals from HA

_____ previous designation as needing   _____ held slots for families in
emergencies housing

_____ solicitation sent to *all* families   _____ other, please specify:

_____ solicitation sent to *some* families   _____

5. Was there a selection preference given to:

_____ family preservation cases

_____ foster care families

_____ no preference

What was the breakdown of the families that received the FUP certificates:

#____ family preservation

#____ foster care

#____ families with children in both

6. Was there a direct liaison person(s) at the housing authority for you to work with on the FUP?

Name _____ Title _____

Are you currently working with this person on other housing/child welfare programs?

_____

7. How did you develop a collaborative relationship with your local Public Housing Authority? What has this relationship included?

_____ sharing staff members   _____ jointly written agreement (MOU)

_____ regular meetings   _____ jointly conducted surveys or
interviews

_____ informal staff gatherings   _____ other (specify)

_____ joint training sessions   _____

8. Have all 1992 FUP certificates been issued to at least one family?

_____

If NO, what is preventing the use of all the certificates?

_____

9. How many children were prevented from going into care because of FUP?

_____

How many children were able to be reunified with their families (out of care) because of FUP?

_____

10. How many of these families have had children returned to care (temporarily or permanently) after moving into their Section 8 housing?

_____

What are the most common reasons that a family was unable to keep their children with them?

_____ new report of abuse/neglect   _____ domestic violence

_____ incorrigible youth   Others:

_____ active substance abuse   _____

_____ mental health problems   _____
      child or parent

11. Have you had any families that were unable to remain in their housing after their certificate had been issued?

_____

What are the most common reasons that a family was unable to remain in their FUP housing?

_____ evicted   _____ family deserted housing

_____ unable to get utilities hooked up   _____ domestic violence

_____ housing condemned   Others:

_____ never actually moved into housing _____

12. How many, if any, FUP families are still active case loads?

_____

Why haven't they been closed out?

____ still in need of general   ____ returned to CPS status

____ entered/re-entered family   Others:
preservation supportive services

_____

____ personal/financial set backs

_____

____ in drug abuse treatment

13. What are the most common/significant supportive services provided to these families?

____ Housing Search Assistance   ____ Transportation Assistance

____ Furniture   ____ Adult Education/Training

____ Moving Assistance   ____ Job Placement Services

____ Health Care   ____ Adult Substance Abuse Treatment

____ Dental Care   ____ Child Substance Abuse Treatment

____ Domestic Violence Support   ____ Parenting Classes

____ Family/Adult Counseling   ____ Child Education (all aspects)

____ Child Counseling   ____ Legal Services

____ Other Mental Health Services   ____ Child Care

____ Food, Clothing, etc.   ____ Money Management/Budgeting

____ Access to entitlements   ____ Other (specify)_____
(AFDC, SSI, WIC, etc.

14. Did you establish a waiting list of FUP-eligible families?

_____

If yes, do you still maintain this list?

_____

How many families are currently on the list?

_____

15. What were the most difficult aspects of getting the FUP off the ground in your community?

_____

16. What were the most effective techniques in administering the FUP?

_____

17. In absence of the FUP program, do you continue to work with the housing authority for families that need housing?

_____

Have you developed any effective local programs and/or preferences?

_____

18. Please send us any written materials that you have used in the FUP program. (i.e. screening forms, referral forms, Memorandum of Understanding between agencies)

Family Unification Program 1st Year Grantees Housing Authority Information Survey

Agency _____

#Units _____

1. Please categorize your agency's general experience with the Family Unification Program.

<table>
<tr><td>Excellent</td><td>Good</td><td>Fair</td><td>Poor</td><td>Very Poor</td></tr>
<tr><td>1</td><td>2</td><td>3</td><td>4</td><td>5 6 7</td></tr>
</table>

2. Did you carry primary responsibility for the FUP?

_____

Were you personally able to award certificates to families for housing that have been referred from the child welfare agency? When do you have to get a supervisor's approval?

_____

3. What other responsibilities do you carry outside FUP? (involved with FSS?)

_____

4. How did you identify families to participate in FUP?

_____ notified all families on waiting list   _____ took referrals from CWA, for families on list

_____ ran advertisements in newspapers

_____ reviewed files for appropriate families   _____ took referrals from CWA, added families to list

5. Was there a direct liaison person(s) at the child welfare agency for you to work with?

Name _____ Title _____

Are you currently working with this person on other child welfare/housing programs?

_____

6. How did you develop a collaborative relationship with your child welfare agency? What did/does this relationship include? Describe. Ongoing?

_____ regular meetings   _____ sharing staff members

_____ informal staff gatherings   _____ joint training sessions

_____ jointly written agreements (MOU)   _____ other (specify)
_____ jointly conducted surveys or
       _____

       interviews

7. What were the bedroom sizes of the FUP certificates issued to you in FY 92?

_____

8. Did you stay exclusively with the bedroom sizes that were issued through FUP or did you substitute as needed from your general Section 8 pool?

_____

How many substitutions were made?

_____ to larger units

_____ to smaller units

Was any eligible family denied a certificate because they didn't fit the allotted sizes?

_____

9. Have all first year certificates been issued to at least one family?

_____

If YES, how long did this "full lease-up" take to accomplish?

_____

If NO, how many remain unassigned, and why?

_____ referred families not on waiting list

_____ not getting referrals from CWA

_____ not identifying enough eligible families

10. Have you had any FUP certificates turn over from the first family they were issued to?

_____

If YES, what are the most common reasons?

____ family moved out of Section 8   ____ increased income, moved to unsubsidized housing

____ unable to find housing w/in time limit   ____ family evicted

____ family deserted housing

11. What is the total number of people that have been housed through the 1992 FUP program?

_____

What is the total number of children?

_____

12. How many have remained intact, with all children at home, during the entire period since receiving their housing?

_____

13. What kind of help did the housing authority offer the families in locating and moving into their Section 8 housing?

____housing search info.   ____household maintenance training

____help with landlords   ____transportation for housing search

____orientation to Section 8   ____help with moving

____help with utilities   ____referrals for social services

____financial assistance   ____other, please specify

14. Are you aware of any FUP families receiving any of these services from outside agencies?

_____

Which ones?

_____

15. How many FUP families enrolled in FSS at the time they got their housing?

_____

How many entered FSS during the three years since they received their FUP housing?

_____

How many FUP families are still in FSS, successfully fulfilling their goals?

_____

16. Did you establish a waiting list for FUP certificates? Is it still maintained?

_____

If YES, how many families are on this list?

_____

17. Did you refer families from the waiting list to the CWA for FUP certification?

YES_____   NO_____

What was the result?

#__ family not in CWA caseload

#__ family certified, housed

#__ family certified, waiting for
    certificate

18. What were the most difficult issues in the FUP for your agency?

____ identifying eligible families   ____ family doesn't follow through on
                                                 appointments

____ inappropriate unit sizes   ____ referred families not on waiting list

____ working with CWA   ____ documenting family eligibility

19. What were the most effective activities in getting FUP off the ground in your community?

____meetings with CWA   ____bypassing list for FUP families

____soliciting families from list   ____certifying CWA referrals

____good communication with CWA

20. In absence of the FUP program, have you been able to house any FUP eligible families using regular Section 8 certificates or vouchers?

_____

Are you working with your child welfare agency to house these families?

_____

21. Have you developed a local preference within the Section 8 program for these families?

_____

22. Please send us any written materials that you have used exclusively in the FUP program. (i.e., screening forms, referral forms, Memorandums of Understanding between agencies)

Survey Results from the 1992 Family Unification Program Sites

827 Section 8 Certificates accounted for:

🏠 **1,275 children** were prevented from going into foster care.

🏠 **869 children** were able to return home from foster care.

🏠 **3,096 people** were housed with these FUP certificates (3.75 people per unit).

🏠 **2,223 children** were housed with these FUP certificates (2.7 children per unit).

Child Welfare Agency Results

29 Child Welfare Agencies (CWA) Reporting:

🏠 1 site (3.4%) has identified **all** FUP families by referrals from the housing authority (HA) to the CWA.

🏠 9 sites (31%) have identified **all** FUP families by referrals from the CWA to the HA.

🏠 17 sites (59%) began the referral process by taking families from the HA waiting list but have since switched to nearly all referrals coming from the CWA.

🏠 19 sites (66%) have allowed families to be referred to the FUP by both the HA and the CWA.

🏠 4 sites (14%) have required that all FUP families come from the pre-existing *closed* HA waiting list for Section 8 housing.

🏠 20 sites (69%) have allowed families identified by the CWA for FUP to be added to the otherwise closed Section 8 waiting lists.

🏠 4 agencies (14%) made preventing the placement of children into foster care their highest priority in identifying FUP eligible families.

🏠 8 agencies (28%) made bringing children home from foster care their highest priority in identifying FUP eligible families.

🏠 17 agencies (59%) did not prioritize either re-unification or prevention of placement higher than the other in identifying FUP eligible families.

🏠 18 Child Welfare Agencies (62%) have no other contact with their HA other than the FUP.

The Child Welfare Agencies were asked what are the most important/common services they provide to FUP families. These were their responses: *

*Percentages do not equal 100 due to multiple answers from respondents.

26 agencies (90%)	On-going Case Management
23 agencies (79%)	Family/Adult Counseling
17 agencies (59%)	Parenting Classes
13 agencies (45%)	Adult Drug Abuse Treatment
11 agencies (38%)	Money Management/Budgeting
8 agencies (28%)	Child Care
7 agencies (24%)	Adult Education/Training
5 agencies (17%)	Access to Entitlement Programs (AFDC, SSI, etc.)
5 agencies (17%)	Domestic Violence Support
4 agencies (14%)	Access to Health Care
4 agencies (14%)	Housing Search Assistance
4 agencies (14%)	Job Placement Services
3 agencies (10%)	Acquiring Basics (Food, Clothing, etc.)
2 agencies (7%)	Help locating/acquiring Furniture
2 agencies (7%)	Transportation Assistance

When CWAs were asked what were the most difficult things about implementing the FUP, these were their responses.

16 agencies (55%)	Referral process between the CWA and HA
15 agencies (52%)	Selecting Eligible Families for FUP
14 agencies (48%)	Communication with the Housing Authority
6 agencies (21%)	Internal CWA problems with the FUP
5 agencies (17%)	Section 8 Waiting list problems
3 agencies (10%)	Property/ Landlord Problems
3 agencies (10%)	Shortage of available Section 8 Housing

When CWAs were asked what are the best aspects of the FUP, these were their responses.

21 agencies (72%)	Having a solid resource for families in a time of crisis
9 agencies (31%)	Working with the housing authority

| 9 agencies (31%) | Other benefits of the FUP |
| 7 agencies (24%) | Learning about housing issues and resources |

14 CWAs (48%) reported that they do have local/state programs that attempt to house similar families to those served in FUP.

14 CWAs (48%) reported that they have no local/state programs that attempt to house similar families to those served in FUP.

Housing Authority Results

🏠 43 Housing Authorities Reporting:

🏠 31 authorities (72%) notified all families on their Section 8 waiting list about the availability of the FUP. Families could then refer themselves to the CWA.

🏠 13 authorities (30%) reviewed their waiting lists and referred appropriate cases to the CWA.

🏠 42 authorities (98%) accepted families referred by CWA that were already on their waiting lists.

🏠 30 authorities (70%) accepted families referred by CWA and added them to their otherwise closed waiting lists.

🏠 40 authorities (93%), after initially reviewing their waiting lists, switched to identifying nearly all FUP families from CWA referrals.

🏠 17 authorities (40%) report working on programs other than FUP with their local Child Welfare Agency.

🏠 26 HAs (61%) reported having a Memorandum of Understanding (MOU) with their collaborating CWA.

🏠 4 HAs (9%) reported not having an MOU with their CWA.

🏠 9 HAs (21%) reported *not knowing* whether they had an MOU with their CWA or not.

🏠 9 HAs (21%) had at least one training session for FUP-involved CWA staff.

🏠 31 HAs (72%) substituted different bedroom sized units than those issued for FUP when necessary to house families.

🏠 12 HAs (28%) issued only the unit sizes that were assigned to the FUP.

🏠 7 HAs (16%) reported having to deny a family from FUP due to these unit size restrictions.

🏠 37 authorities (86%) have issued every FUP certificate they have received to at least one family.

🏠 6 authorities (14%) of HA still have unissued FUP certificates as of March 1995.

This is a breakdown of the time spent issuing all certificates to one family.

One to three months	5 HA	(12%)
Three to six months	6 HA	(14%)
Six to nine months	6 HA	(14%)
Nine to twelve months	10 HA	(23%)
One year to 18 months	5 HA	(12%)
Over 18 months	9 HA	(21%)

(includes those currently with unissued certificates.)

When asked what support services the HA offers FUP families, these were the responses:

37 authorities	(86%)	Housing search information
25 authorities	(58%)	Referrals for social services
15 authorities	(34%)	Help negotiating with landlords
4 authorities	(9%)	Financial assistance
3 authorities	(7%)	Help with utilities
3 authorities	(7%)	Household maintenance training

22 HAs (51%) reported having FUP waiting lists at some time since the program began.

17 HAs (40%) currently have a waiting list for the FUP.

When HAs were asked what are the most difficult aspects of implementing the FUP, these were the responses:

20 HAs (47%)	Working with the child welfare agency
17 HAs (40%)	Other program aspects
13 HAs (30%)	Identifying eligible families
10 HAs (23%)	Documenting family eligibility
6 HAs (14%)	Families not following through

| 4 HAs (9%) | Unit size problems |
| 3 HAs (7%) | Waiting list issues |

When HAs were asked what are the best aspects of the FUP, these were their responses:

30 HAs (70%)	Providing an excellent program for needy families
20 HAs (47%)	Crucial timing of the housing for families in crisis
15 HAs (35%)	Developing good communication with CWA
7 HAs (16%)	Learning about CWA issues
7 HAs (16%)	Other program aspects

8 HAs (19%) have a local preference within their Section 8 program to serve families similar to those in FUP.

21 HAs (49%) have some type of local program that aims to house families similar to those in FUP.

7 HAs (17%) report having no programs other than FUP that house this population of families.

Appendix E

CWLA's Model Memorandum of Understanding for Child Welfare/Housing Collaborations

Memorandum of Understanding
Family Unification Program 1996

OUTLINE

Goals for the Program

(1) Eligibility Criteria for Section 8 Certificates under the Family Unification Program (FUP)

(2) Role and Responsibilities of Housing Authority (HA) in Selecting Families

(3) Role and Responsibilities of Child Welfare Agency (CWA) in Certifying Families

(4) Procedures for Use of HA Waiting List for Section 8 Rental Assistance

(5) HA Tenant Selection of Families

(6) Service Plan for Families Certified for the Family Unification Program

(7) Community Resources

(8) Housing and Financial Assistance for FUP families

(9) Family Unification Program Project Advisory Committee

(10) Coordination of FUP with other HUD and HHS Housing and Service Programs

(11)   Cross Training of HA and CWA Program Staff Members

(12)   Family Unification Program Hearing/Grievance Procedure

(13)   CWA and HA Reporting on Families in the Family Unification Program

(14)   Tenant Briefing Sessions

Appendix A - PROCEDURES for: Outreach and Referral for Section 8 FUP Program

Appendix B - Outreach and Referral letters, "A", "B", "C", "D", "E" for FUP program

FY 1995

MEMORANDUM of UNDERSTANDING

This Memorandum of Understanding is executed between the_____Housing Authority and the_____Child Welfare Agency regarding the Family Unification Program.

A. The (Housing Authority) and the (Child Welfare Agency) have agreed to the following goals for the Family Unification Program:

- To ensure that rental assistance payments help families who are involved with the child welfare system find affordable and decent housing in a safe and supportive environment; and

- To ensure that children who remain with their families or who are reunited with their families are safe and secure and not subject to neglect as a result of homelessness or inadequate housing.

B. The (Housing Authority) and the (Child Welfare Agency) also have agreed to work together to achieve the following goals to the maximum extent possible:

- To empower families to resolve their own problems, effectively utilize service systems, and advocate for their children with schools, public and private agencies, and other community institutions;

- To ensure that family problems are identified as early as possible and engage families in a change process to remedy these problems;

- To involve the community in identifying community-based services, expand those services, and where necessary, advocate for new service programs, and

- To prevent child abuse and neglect and the unnecessary separation of children from their families.

C. The program will be deemed successful if it meets the following standards:

- At least 90% of the children threatened with separation from their families or reunited with their families, remain together in their subsidized unit for six months;

🏠 During the first year after unification: at least 75% of the children threatened with separation from their families or reunited with their families remain together in their subsidized unit for one year.

🏠 Two years after the families move to a Section 8 subsidized unit after threat of separation or the date of family reunification in the case of previous out-of-home placement, at least 65% of the children threatened with separation from their families or families reunified will be together whether or not they continue living in subsidized housing.

1. Eligibility Criteria for Family Unification Program (FUP) Certificates—Family

Unification eligibility is based on a family fitting the following criteria, from the NOFA dated May 2, 1996:

a. The public child welfare agency has certified a family for whom the lack of adequate housing* is a primary factor in the imminent placement of a family's child or children in out-of-home care, or in the delay in reuniting a child(ren) who are in out-of-home care with the family; and

b. The housing authority has determined this family is eligible for the Section 8 rental assistance (note details of criteria in NOFA).

2. The Role and Responsibilities of the Housing Agency (HA) in the Selection of Families for the Family Unification Program.

a. Determine whether the families referred by the CWA are eligible for any Section 8 housing, HA *does not re-determine eligibility for FUP program.*

b. The HA will review the existing Section 8 waiting list to identify families that may be eligible for the Family Unification Program, continue to review new applicants for the Section 8 program, and refer the families on the Section 8 waiting list to the CWA for a determination of whether the family meets eligibility requirements.

c. Processing of housing subsidies and distribution to families in the order referred.

d. Make changes in administrative and equal opportunity plan where necessary;

e. Maintain quality program data for future program evaluation;

f. If Section 8 assistance to any FUP family is terminated, the certificate will be re- issued to another eligible family. The HA guarantees that number of Section 8 Certificates will be available to FUP families;

---

* Lack of adequate housing means a situation in which a family is living in substandard housing or is or will be involuntarily displaced from a housing unit.

g. The HA will expedite the process for third party verification of a family's income and eligibility to the maximum extent possible. The HA will complete the third part verification while the family is searching for a unit and will use oral verification where applicable.

3. *The Role and Responsibilities of the Child Welfare Agency (CWA) in the Certification of Families for the Family Unification Program*

a. Establish and implement a system to identify eligible families within the agency's caseload and reviewing referrals from the HA; CWA is responsible for certifying families eligible for FUP.

b. Develop procedures for referring FUP eligible families to the HA and provide written certification to the HA that a family qualifies for the FUP.

c. Commit staff to ensure that eligible families are identified and the certification process is completed in a timely manner.

d. CWA agrees to maintain relevant data and provide written information as requested for program evaluation.

4. *Procedure for Use of the HA Waiting List for Section 8 Rental Assistance*

a. The HA will first review its list to determine if there are any CWA-referred families already on the list who may be eligible.

b. In those instances where the Housing Authority waiting list is closed, and the waiting lists have been exhausted for FUP families, the HA may open the list for Family Unification Program eligible families only. These families may be referred by the CWA, referred by private service providers, or families may refer themselves.

c. Once a list of FUP eligible families has been made, FUP certificates will be disbursed in the rank order of the Section 8 waiting list;

d. See Appendix A—Procedures for Outreach and Referral letters for Section 8 FUP Family Unification Program.

e. Appendix B—Outreach and Referral letters "A","B","C","D","E" for FUP.

5. *HA Tenant Selection of Families*

Families on the Eligibility List for the Family Unification Program that also qualify for Section 8 Certificates will be offered housing based on:

a. Their rank order on the Section 8 waiting list, or the order in which they were referred, and

b. Availability of a Family Unification Program Section 8 Certificate of the budget allotment needed.

6. Service Plan for Families Certified for the Family Unification Program

a. For each certified family whose child(ren) is at imminent risk of placement in out-of-home care, CWA will include within the existing service plan for the family, or as a separate service plan, housing services and supportive services as needed. The family shall participate in the development and implementation of the service plan, but failure to participate will not jeopardize Section 8 subsidy.

b. For each certified family whose child(ren) is in placement in out-of-home care, CWA shall include within the existing service plan or as a separate plan: the anticipated date of the child's return to the parent, the housing services needed, and the supportive services needed. The family shall participate in the development and implementation of the service plan, but failure to participate will not jeopardize Section 8 subsidy.

c. Upon location of the family in housing through the Family Unification Program, CWA shall assist the family in identifying ongoing service needs and shall ensure that the family has been referred to community resources that can assist the family in meeting those needs. CWA will address such issues as: (1) services to enable parents to meet the basic care needs of the child(ren); (2) the healthy and appropriate development of the child(ren); (3) maximizing safety within the home (including issues of domestic violence); and (4) services to enhance economic and social self-sufficiency.

7. Community Resources

The CWA case manager will be responsible for the delivery of services as developed with the family and outlined in the families' Service Plan. These services may include, but not be limited to direct provision or referral to: case management/counseling; child care; adult education; parenting skill training; vocational training; mental and physical health care; substance abuse testing and treatment; and family advocacy.

8. Housing and Financial Assistance to Family Unification Program Families

The CWA and the HA will jointly prepare and implement, where feasible, an emergency services plan to new FUP families which may include, but are not limited to the following: Housing search and financial assistance, such as moving expenses, security deposits, rental/utility arrearage payments and emergency health, welfare and legal services.

9. Family Unification Program Project Advisory Committee

The *Housing Authority* and the *Child Welfare Agency* will jointly establish and staff a community-based Family Unification Program Project Advisory Committee (PAC), made up of public and private agencies involved in child and family services and other organizations or persons as appropriate to meet program goals.

The Project Advisory Committee will meet regularly to:

a. review reports on program utilization, family service needs, and project evaluation. HA and CWA will designate staff to provide liaison between the two agencies and the cooperating service network for the Family Unification Program.

b. recommend service program changes or additions to meet needs of families in the FUP.

10. Coordination of Family Unification Program with other HUD- and HHS-funded Programs

The HA and CWA will coordinate FUP service programs with other HHS funded programs and housing programs such as the HUD Family Self-Sufficiency Program, so that successful family unification may be achieved using all available resources.

11. Cross Training of HA and CWA Staff

The HA will offer training to designated CWA staff as it relates to HA Section 8 Program Application Procedures and eligibility requirements. Cross training from the CWA will be offered to housing authority staff to describe CWA mandates and procedures regarding family preservation and family unification. Training topics will include but not limited to, interagency referrals, certification of eligible families and timely provisions of services.

12. Family Unification Program Hearing/Grievance Procedure

a. All persons applying to or enrolled in the Family Unification Program can request an informal hearing from the HA on their Section 8 application.

b. The HA is responsible for defending its eligibility decisions pertaining to the family's eligibility for Section 8 rental assistance. Section 8 informal hearing procedures will be utilized.

c. The CWA is responsible for defending its FUP family eligibility determinations.

d. The procedure to be used in these instances shall be the same as currently in effect for Section 8 Participants, as set forth in the approved Section 8 Housing Program Administrative Plan.

13. CWA and HA Reporting on Families in the Family Unification Program

a. Both HA and CWA will maintain and update statistical reports on families in the program. This data will be made available to the FUP Advisory Committee, HUD or HHS, CWLA and any official HUD evaluation.

b. The reports will include demographic data, family service needs, service utilization information and unification experience.

c. Reports will be prepared on initial occupancy on the families and at three-month intervals for at least two years.

14. Tenant Briefing Sessions

The HA application and apartment leasing process will provide briefing sessions for FUP certified tenants. These meetings may include but not be limited to the following: Apartment Search techniques, lease negotiations, housing discrimination, housing quality standards, tenants rights and responsibilities, and, where appropriate, apartment maintenance, housekeeping and budgeting.

Appendix A—Procedures For: Outreach and Referral, Section 8 FUP Program

Appendix B—Outreach and Referral Letters "A," "B," "C," "D," "E" for FUP Program

HA's Outreach and Referral Efforts for Selection of Family Unification Program Participants

a. The HA will use FORM "E" for identifying potential FUP participants from their existing and new Section 8 applicants. Those families found to be eligible for housing assistance with a Federal Preference due to: Being homeless; living in substandard housing; or, being involuntarily displaced, and requesting to participate in the Family Unification Program will be referred to the CWA using FORM "B."

The HA will send the "release of information" from FORM "E" for each referred family that they include in FORM B.

a. FORM "B" will be returned from the CWA with verification of each families status. Families that have been verified to fit all FUP criteria will be placed on a Family Unification Program eligibility list and will have a coded entry next to their name on the Section 8 established waiting list.

b. Those families that are deemed INELIGIBLE by the CWA on FORM "B" will be notified by the Housing Authority in writing that their application to participate in the Family Unification Program has been denied on grounds of program eligibility, but their position on the Section 8 waiting list is safely retained.

c. The HA will review the files of all families referred to them from the CWA, on FORM "A." The status of each family will be recorded and the original FORM "A" will be returned to the CWA. Those families that are currently on the Section 8 waiting list will be placed on the Family Unification list and a coded entry will be placed next to their name on the Section 8 list.

Those families that are eligible for housing but not currently on the waiting list, will be called into the HA office and placed on both the general Section 8 list (with a coded entry) and the FUP list. The status of all families approved by the HA will be documented to the CWA on FORM "C."

Those families that are ineligible will be notified in writing by the CWA that they do not qualify for Section 8 housing due to housing authority criteria and are therefore ineligible for the FUP. In that notification will be a statement of the right to appeal the decision, as set forth in the Agency Administrative Plan. The HA is responsible for defending its eligibility decisions as to the family's programmatic eligibility for the Section 8 rental certificates. Section 8 informal housing procedures will be utilized.

The Outreach and Referral Efforts of the CWA for the Family Unification Program among All Families Served by That Agency

a. CWA will implement an in-house review of all existing and in-coming child welfare families. FORM "D" will be used as a outreach effort to these families at their in-take session or their regular meeting with their caseworker. All families that are found to be eligible for the FUP under the child welfare criteria: imminent risk of placement or delay in reunification due to inadequate housing; will be referred to the HA for Section 8 verification on FORM "A." The "release of information" (part of FORM "D") will be included for each family listed on FORM "A."

b. FORM "A" will be returned from the HA indicating the status of each family.

Those families that are deemed eligible by the HA will be added to the general Section 8 list (if necessary) with a coded entry and all eligible families will be added to the Family Unification list. Documentation of the status of these families will be sent to the CWA on FORM "C."

c. Families (from FORM "A") deemed INELIGIBLE by the HA will be notified in writing that they are ineligible for Section 8 housing due to Housing Authority criteria, and are therefore ineligible for Family Unification. In that notification will be a statement of the right to appeal the decision, as set forth in the Agency Administrative Plan. The HA is responsible for defending its eligibility decisions as to the family's programmatic eligibility for the Section 8 rental certificates. Section 8 informal housing procedures will be utilized.

d. Families referred to the CWA from the HA on FORM "B" will be reviewed for child welfare criteria. The status of each family will be recorded and the original FORM "B" will be returned to the HA. Those families that meet all FUP requirements will be placed on the FUP list, this will be documented to the CWA on FORM "C."

Those families (from FORM "B") that are deemed INELIGIBLE by the CWA, will be notified in writing by the HA that their application to participate in the Family Unification Program has been denied on grounds of program eligibility, but their position on the Section 8 waiting list is safely retained.

Referral Letter from the Child Welfare Agency to the Housing Authority

FORM "A"

DATE:

TO: HA

FROM: CWA

Please see the attached forms. We are referring the listed families to you from our active case loads. Note the attached release of information form for each family. They have each been determined to fulfill the child welfare criteria for the Family Unification Program. Please verify whether they are currently on the Section 8 waiting list, whether they are eligible to be placed on the list, or if they are ineligible for Section 8 housing. Please add the eligible families to the list that are not currently on it. Check the appropriate column, make a copy of the list for your files and return the original form to the CWA.

Please send the CWA the form of confirmation (FORM C) for each of these families that is granted a Section 8 certificate through the Family Unification Program.

If you have any questions about this process please call, _____ at CWA.

Questions about particular families should be directed to their case worker as noted on the form.

Thank You.

CWA-Eligible Families for Family Unification Program (Form "A")

Name _____ Address, Phone Contact _____ Social Security Number _____ Case Worker: Name & Number _____	Family Currently on Section 8 list	Family eligible & will be placed on list	Family NOT eligible for Section 8
1.			
2.			
3.			
4.			
5.			
6.			

Referral from Housing Authority to Child Welfare Agency

FORM "B"

DATE:

TO: HA

FROM: CWA

Please see the attached form. We are referring these families for possible participation in the Family Unification Program. Note the attached release of information Each of these families are currently on the Section 8 waiting list. Please verify if they are among your open cases and if they qualify for the Family Unification Program under the child welfare criteria. Please check the appropriate column, make a copy of the form for your records, and return this form to the HA. Families on this list that are verified by you will be granted a slot in the Family Unification Program.

A form of confirmation (FORM C) will be sent for each family that is issued a Section 8 certificate through this program. If you have any questions about this process please call _____ at the HA. Questions concerning individual families should be directed to their caseworker who is indicated in the form.

Thank You.

Families from HA: On Section 8 List (Form "B")

Name _____ Address, Phone Contact _____ Social Security Number _____ Case Worker: Name & Number _____	Family at imminent risk of separation by housing	Family being kept apart by housing	Family NOT an active case with CWA
1.			
2.			
3.			
4.			
5.			
6.			

Notification of Family Unification Program Participation

FORM "C"

TO: CWA

FROM: HA

RE: CONFIRMATION OF A REFERRED FAMILY'S PARTICIPATION

Head Of Household Name: _____

Current Address: _____

Phone Contact: _____

Date Family Placed On Fup List _____

And Approximate Rank On List _____

Or Date Section 8 Certificate Granted: _____

Certificate Bedroom Size Needed: _____

Certificate Bedroom Size Granted: _____

Housing Authority Contact: _____

Contact Phone # _____

The above noted family has been verified to be eligible for the Family Unification Program by both the HA and the CWA. They have either been placed on the FUP waiting list or have already been granted a FUP certificate (as noted). If you have any questions or concerns about this family or about the Family Unification program in general, please contact as the HA worker as noted above.

Thank You.

FORM "D"

Introductory Letter CWA Families for the Family Unification Program

FAMILY UNIFICATION PROGRAM

The Housing Authority of _____ may be able to assist you with your housing needs on an emergency basis if you believe that you and your children may be separated from each other due to lack of adequate housing, or if the return of your children to you from placement away from your family is being delayed because you do not have adequate housing. In order to know if you are eligible for housing for the reasons stated above through the Family Unification Program, please fill out the form below and leave it with your CWA caseworker.

<u>**Your participation in this process is strictly voluntary and any existing position on the Section 8 waiting list will not be jeopardized!**</u>

Upon receipt of the form, your housing needs will be evaluated by the CWA. If you meet the criteria for the Program, we will notify the Housing Authority—and request that they determine your eligibility for Section 8 assisted housing. If you are eligible for Section 8 assisted housing, your name will be placed on a waiting list for a Family Unification Program Section 8 Certificate, and this will not adversely affect an existing position on the Section 8 Program waiting list. Participation in the program is based on both eligibility and position on the Section 8 waiting list. Eligibility is not a guarantee that you will receive immediate housing.

FORM "D"

I hereby request that the CWA review my circumstances, and if I qualify for the Family Unification Program, certify the same to the (Housing Authority).

(PLEASE PRINT)

Name _____

Address _____

City, State, Zip _____

Telephone ( ) _____

Signature _____

Date _____

Social Security Number _____

FORM "E"

Introductory Letter to Section 8 Applicants at HA (City, County, State) Family Unification Program

The (Housing Authority) may be able to assist you with your housing needs through a new Family Unification Program. This program may help you if you believe that you and your children may be separated from each other due to lack of adequate housing, or if the return of your children to you from placement outside of your family unit is being delayed because you do not have adequate housing. If you think you may qualify for the program, please fill out and mail the form below to your CWA caseworker.

Your participation in this process is strictly voluntary and your position on the Section 8 waiting list will be not be jeopardized!

If the CWA certifies that your family meets the criteria for the Family Unification Program, AND YOU ARE ALSO FOUND ELIGIBLE FOR ASSISTED HOUSING UNDER THE GUIDELINES ESTABLISHED BY HUD FOR THE SECTION 8 PROGRAM, you will be placed on a waiting list for a Family Unification Program Section 8 Certificate, as well as on the waiting list for a regular Section 8 Certificate/Voucher. Although this will not guarantee housing for you, it may increase the opportunity for you and your family to receive rental assistance.

FORM "E"

I hereby request that the CWA review my circumstances, and if I qualify for the Family Unification Program, certify the same to the Housing Authority of _____.

(PLEASE PRINT)

Name _____

Address _____

City, State, Zip _____

Telephone (   ) _____

Signature _____

Date _____

Social Security Number _____

Appendix F

Program Protocols, New Jersey Department of Community Affairs

NEW JERSEY DEPARTMENT OF COMMUNITY AFFAIRS
DIVISION OF HOUSING AND COMMUNITY RESOURCES
and the
NEW JERSEY DEPARTMENT OF HUMAN SERVICES
DIVISION OF YOUTH AND FAMILY SERVICES

FAMILY UNIFICATION PROGRAM
PROTOCOL

The Family Unification Program is a cooperative program between the Department of Community Affairs (DCA), the "Local Housing Agency" in Newark, Jersey City, Lakewood and Orange, and the Division of Youth and Family Services (DYFS) to provide Section 8 Housing Certificates to eligible families. Eligibility for the program is based on the following criteria:

Eligibilty Criteria

1.   A family must lack adequate housing which is the primary factor for the imminent placement of the family's child, or children in out-of-home placement or the delay of discharge of a child, or children, to the family from out-of-home placement.

2.   The family must meet Section 8 eligibility criteria, as determined by the Housing Agency or DCA.

The Section 8 Housing Certificates are limited in this program and once assigned to a family are extremely difficult to recapture and reassign to another family. Also, families will utilize these certificates for at least 5 years. Since the purpose of this program is the reunification of children and families, or the prevention of family break-up, priority will be given to families where preservation is a long term realistic goal. For this reason, referrals should be made for those families that would most benefit from the program. This would include:

o   Families with young children.

o   Families that have a good history of paying their bills.

o   Families that do not have other contributing factors, such as substance abuse issues, which would prevent family reunification or family preservation.

FAMILY UNIFICATION PROGRAM

REFERRAL PROTOCOL

1. Based on the Eligibility Criteria, a family is identified as a potential referral for Family Unification.

2. The DYFS caseworker will discuss the family's situation with the supervisor. If there is agreement that the family appears to be a good candidate for the Family Unification Program (FUP), a referral form and certification form will be completed, signed by the supervisor and given to the respective DYFS county FUP liaison.

3. The DYFS FUP liaison will review all of the referrals and send the highest priority referrals to the Housing Agency/DCA, and will provide concrete proof of return of the child(ren) to the head of household, for example, recommendation of Child Placement Review Board.

4. The Housing Agency/DCA will make the final determination regarding Section 8 eligiblity and will advise the FUP liaison about each case referral, within 14 days.

5. The DYFS FUP liason will advise the DYFS caseworker and/or the supervisor regarding the family's eligiblity for the Section 8 Program.

6. Before a family has been found eligible, the DYFS FUP liaison will provide a copy of a general family case plan tailored to the objectives of the program to the Housing Agency/DCA representative. The staff from these agencies are very knowledgeable about housing issues, and can provide expertise in those areas.

7. If a program participant chooses to excerise "portability" under the Section 8 Housing Program, the Housing Agency/DCA will advise the DYFS FUP liaison immediately.

8. In counties that have established Family Self-Sufficiency Programs, the DYFS FUP liaison and housing representative will encourage client participation in the program, as appropriate. In counties that do not currently administer a Family Self-Sufficiency Program, the DYFS FUP liason will continue to be responsible for providing or linking participants to other needed services.

9. A FUP case will not be closed without the mutual consent of DYFS and the Housing Agency/DCA.

10. If there is a need for a conflict resolution, the DYFS FUP liaison and Section 8 Supervisor will meet and attempt to resolve the situation. If there is no agreement, the District Office Manager and Section 8 Supervisor will meet to resolve the conflict. If a resolution cannot be negotiated the case will be presented to the Regional staff from both divisions to negotiate a solution. If there is still no resolution, the case will be presented to the DYFS and DCA statewide FUP liaisons for a final decision.

Appendix G

Assessment Tool for Screening Families St. Louis, Missouri

Family Unification Assessment

In 1991, the St. Louis Lawyers' Project on Homelessness and Inadequate Housing formed a Subcommittee on Foster Care and Inadequate Housing. The focus of the Subcommittee was families whose children have been placed in care or who are at risk of placement due to homelessness or inadequate housing. Current estimates of the Division of Family Services indicate that in 1993, there were over 200 children placed in foster care because of inadequate housing.

The Subcommittee strives to link agencies serving this population, including the City of St. Louis' Division of Family Services, St. Louis Housing Authority, Juvenile Court, service providers and child advocates. When St. Louis received Section 8 certificates under a new federal program, the Subcommittee was able to coordinate efforts of the agencies to identify and serve eligible families.

The federal program providing the certificates was the Family Unification Act, passed as a part of the 1990 National Affordable Housing Act. Families designated for receiving certificates are those at risk of losing their children to foster care, or whose children have been placed in care primarily due to housing issues.

The City of St. Louis is hoping to receive additional Section 8 certificates this year. To better serve the families eligible to participate, the Subcommittee has developed guidelines to identify families. Attached is a review of the selection process, and the assessment form which will be utilized by the Division of Family Services.

Procedure for Family Assessment and Selection

Representatives from the Division of Family Services-City of St. Louis, St. Louis Housing Authority, Juvenile Court and the Subcommittee of Foster Care and Inadequate Housing have met to discuss proposals for assessing and choosing families for participation under the Family Unification Act (the Act). This committee has approved a form for assessing families' eligibility for receiving housing. The following guidelines set forth the procedure which is proposed for choosing families:

1. A list of families who may be eligible will be chosen initially by social service workers at the Division of Family Services-City of St. Louis, and by Juvenile Court.

2. For each of the families listed, assessment forms will be complete.

3. A selection team or committee will be to review each of the assessment forms.

4. The selection team will make the final decision regarding the families chosen for participation in the Family Unification Act.

Because of the collaborative effort which has led to the above-proposed guidelines and to the development of the assessment form, it is the opinion of this committee that the same collaboration should be utilized in choosing those families who will receive housing under the Act. The committee therefore proposes that representatives from each of the agencies who participated in the drafting process be represented in a selection team, who will make the final decision regarding a family's eligibility for participation: The Division of Family Services-City of St. Louis; St. Louis Housing Authority; Juvenile Court for the City of St. Louis. It is anticipated that each team representative will be chosen by the appropriate agency.

Assessment Form for Family Unification Applicants

For use by Division of Family Services only.

Name: _____

Address: _____

Telephone Number: _____ Message Phone: _____

Date of Birth: _____ DCN _____

Income: _____

Source of Income: _____

Children of Applicant: _____

Name	Race/Sex	Date of Birth	DCN	Will child reside in home?
1.				
2.				
3.				
4.				
5.				
6.				
7.				
8.				
9.				
10.				

Is the family currently involved with Juvenile Court? _____

Name and Telephone Number of DJO: _____

Name of Referring Social Service Worker: _____

Telephone Number: _____

Signature of Immediate Supervisor: _____

Assessment

1. Are the applicant and his/her family currently homeless or at risk of losing his/her home?

_____

2. Where is the applicant currently staying?

_____

3. Are the children currently in foster care?

_____

4. If the children are not currently in foster care, are the children at risk of placement as a result of homelessness or substandard living conditions?

_____

5. If the children are currently in care, what are the reasons (other than lack of housing) which are preventing their return to their natural parents?

_____

6. Does the applicant receive supportive services from any community resources other than DFS or Juvenile Court?

_____

If yes, what is the name of the resource and the name of a contact person?

_____

7. Is the applicant currently using alcohol or any chemical substance? Is the applicant currently taking medication?

_____

Type and frequency _____

Is the applicant currently enrolled in a treatment program, or has applicant received treatment in the past?

_____

Name of treatment program and contact person: _____

Estimated date of program completion:

_____

Has applicant ever been recommended to a treatment program, but refused treatment?

_____

Are their supportive services, such as AA/NA? Has the applicant obtained any of these services?

_____

8. Has the applicant lived independently in the past (been responsible for paying rent and utilities for a family residence)?

_____

a. If yes, where did the applicant live?

_____

b. Whose name was on the lease, or who was the homeowner?

_____

c. If the applicant paid rent and utilities to a friend or family member to maintain a residence, what were the name and address of the payee?

_____

9. Does the applicant have outstanding balances on his/her utility bills?

_____

If yes, how much is owed to:

Laclede Gas_____

Union Electric _____

Verification by Housing Authority _____

10. Has the applicant been involuntarily displaced through any of the following means:

Is not presently living in standard, permanent replacement housing, or will be involuntarily displaced within six months of the date of certification?

Is living in substandard housing and/or is a homeless family who lacks a fixed, regular and adequate night time residence?

Is paying more than fifty percent of family income for rent?

11. Has the applicant received a high school diploma or G.E.D. certificate? If applicant has answered no, is he/she currently enrolled in a G.E.D. program, and if so, where?

_____

12. Is the applicant currently enrolled in FUTURES or an equivalent training program? If applicant has answered yes, where?

_____

Appendix H

Inter-agency Referral Form, San Jose, California

Santa Clara County   Social Services Agency

FAMILY UNIFICATION PROGRAM (FUP)
REFERRAL FROM DFCS TO HOUSING AUTHORITY

SECTION I   (To be completed by Child Welfare Staff)

CASE NAME: _____   TELEPHONE NUMBER: _____

CLIENT NAME: _____   SSN: _____

CASE NUMBER: _____

NUMBER OF CHILDREN

Male: _____   Ages: _____

Female: _____   Ages: _____

I certify that the above family is currently receiving Child Welfare Services from: (please check one only)

FAMILY REUNIFICATION   FAMILY MAINTENANCE
- [ ] Court Ordered (FRC)   - [ ] Court Ordered (FMC)
- [ ] Voluntary (VFR)   - [ ] Informal Supervision (IS)
                                         - [ ] Voluntary (VFM)

The family is referred to the Family Unification Program because: (please check the appropriate reason)

- [ ] Lack of adequate housing is a primary factor which may cause the separation or imminent separation of the child(ren) from the family.

- [ ] Lack of adequate housing is a primary factor which may delay the discharge of this child(ren) to the family from out-of-house care.

CHILD WELFARE SOCIAL WORKER: _____   DISTRICT NUMBER: _____

PHONE NUMBER: (   ) _____   FAX NUMBER: (   ) _____

REFERRAL APPROVED: **William Drennan, Family Preservation Program Specialist**

PHONE NUMBER: (408) 441-5275   FAX NUMBER: (408) 441-7913

_____   _____
(Signature of FPP Specialist)   (Date)

FAMILY UNIFICATION PROGRAM (FUP) CERTIFICATION OF ELIGIBILITY

SECTION II   (To be completed by Housing Authority Staff)

Client Seen On _____ (Month/Day/Year)	Family Unification Eligible? ☐ Yes ☐ No	FUP Interagency I.D. # _____

If not eligible, explain: _____
_____

Critical Emergent Need (explain): _____

HOUSING CERTIFICATE ISSUED (Month/Day/Year): _____

HOUSING AUTHORITY APPROVAL: **Sandi Douglas, Community Services Manager**

PHONE NUMBER: (408) 993-3064   FAX NUMBER: (408) 971-7873

_____   _____
(Signature of Housing Authority Manager)   (Date)

Please return one copy to DFCS Family Preservation Program Specialist, 1725 Technology Dr., San Jose, CA 95110.

SC 490 (FP) - 8/94

Appendix I

UD's Federal Housing Preferences

These previously mandated regulations have been repealed for FY 1996 and FY 1997. Local housing agencies now have the option whether to use all, some, or none of these preference categories. Many housing agencies already HAVE amended parts of these preferences for their local programs. Child welfare professionals and other advocates should be aware of these federal regulations so that they are familiar with these long-standing program criteria and can discuss current preference changes with housing agency staff.

Programs Covered by the Preference Rules

- 🏠 Section 8 Housing Assistance Payments Program for New Construction

- 🏠 Section 8 Housing Assistance Payments Program for Substantial Rehabilitation

- 🏠 Section 8 Housing Assistance Payments Program-Existing Housing-Special Procedures for Moderate Rehabilitation-Program Development and Operation

- 🏠 Section 8 Housing Assistance Payments Program-State Housing Agencies

- 🏠 Section 8 Housing Assistance Payments Program, New Construction Set-Aside for Section 515 Rural Rental Housing Projects

- 🏠 Loans for Housing for the Elderly

- 🏠 Section 8 Housing Assistance Payments Program—Special Allocations—Additional Assistance Programs for Projects with HUD-Insured and HUD-Held Mortgages

- 🏠 Supportive Housing for the Elderly

- 🏠 Low Rent Housing Homeownership Opportunities

- 🏠 Indian Housing

- 🏠 Section 5(h) Homeownership Program

- 🏠 Public Housing

Section 8 Certificate and Voucher Programs Conforming Rule: Admissions

- 🏠 Section 8 Rental Certificates
- 🏠 Section 8 Rental Vouchers

Note: This information is taken from a "Briefing on HUD's Preference Rules," held on Thursday, July 14, 1994.

Examples of Programs Not Covered by the Preference Rules

🏠 HOME

🏠 Low Income Housing Tax Credits

What Are the Federal Preferences?

🏠 *Families who have been involuntarily displaced and are not living in standard, permanent replacement housing or families who will be involuntarily displaced within six months.*

Displacement may result from:

- Disaster, such as a fire or flood

- Government action or action of a housing owner other than a rent increase

- Domestic violence

- Threat of reprisal for providing information on criminal activity to a law enforcement agency

- Hate crime

- The current unit of a disabled resident is inaccessible

🏠 *Families who are living in substandard housing (including families that are homeless or living in a shelter for the homeless). Housing may be substandard if it does not have:*

- Operable indoor plumbing

- Usable indoor flush toilet for exclusive use of a family

- Usable indoor bathtub or shower for the exclusive use of a family

- Electricity, or adequate, safe electrical service

- Safe or adequate source of heat

🏠 *Families who are paying more than 50 percent of family income for rent.*

In all cases, a family's claim for a Federal Preference must be verified. Verification procedures for owners are specified in the rule, and vary by which preference is being claimed. For HA administered programs, verification procedures are locally determined.

There Are Three Types of Preferences

Federal Preferences

Federal preferences are prescribed by Federal law and are *required* to be used in the selection process.

Ranking Preferences

Ranking preferences *may* be established for use in selecting among applicants that qualify for Federal preferences; they are locally determined.

Local Preferences

Local preferences may be established for selecting among applicants without regard to their Federal preference status; they are also locally determined. If a PHA chooses to use local preferences, such local preferences must be established after the PHA has held public hearings to establish preferences that respond to local housing needs and priorities.

Percent of New Admissions Each Year That Must Be Federal Preference Holders and Percent That May Be Chosen Based on Local Preferences

Program	Minimum % Federal Preference Holders	Maximum % Local Preference Holders
Public housing (including public housing homeownership programs)	50	50
Indian housing	70	30
Section 8—Project Based (and other project based programs)	70	30
Section 8—Certificates and Vouchers	90	10

Appendix J

Preliminary Data on the Needs and Characteristics of Families Housed through the Family Unification Program

Vanderbilt Institute for Public Policy Studies
Center for Mental Health Policy
1609 Connecticut Avenue, NW, Suite 401
Washington, DC 20009

Debra J. Rog, Ph.D., Principal Investigator
Ariana Gilbert, M.P.P., Project Coordinator
Ezell Lundy, B.A., Research Assistant

December 1995

This research is funded through the Massachusetts General Hospital with funds from the Robert Wood Johnson Foundation.

Analyses in progress; please contact Vanderbilt before citing data for external use.

Family Unification Program Preliminary Data

I.   OVERVIEW OF THE EVALUATION SCOPE

🏠 The evaluation focuses on FY 1993 program sites (sites funded in the second year).

🏠 Data are collected from 35 Housing Agencies and 39 Child Welfare Agencies located in 10 states.

🏠 All families referred to and housed through FY 1993 program funds are included in the Management Information System.

II.   DESCRIPTION OF THE PRELIMINARY DATA SET

🏠 All FY 1993 FUP sites have submitted some data.

🏠 All data reported were received by Vanderbilt as of 12/1/95.

🏠 955 families have public housing lease-up data

(approximately 60% of the FY 1993 Section 8 certificates).

🏠 639 leased-up families also have child welfare referral data

(approximately 40% of the FY 1993 Section 8 certificates).

III.   DEMOGRAPHIC CHARACTERISTICS

Total Families Housed *

     N=955

Female-Headed	85%
Average Age of Primary Parent	31 years
Race/Ethnicity of Primary Parent	
White	33%
Black	48%
Hispanic	17%
Average # Children	2.6 children
Families with More than 3 Children	23%
Families with a Child Under 1 Year	18%
Families with a Child Under 3 Years	52%

* Includes all families on whom we have received a PHA Lease-Up/50058 Form as of 12/1/95.

IV.   ELIGIBILITY INFORMATION

	Total Families Housed* N=639
Where Primary Parent Was Living at Referral:	
With Friend/Relative	46%
Own Residence	27%
Shelter (non-Domestic Violence)	10%
Transitional Housing	6%
Substance Abuse/Mental Health Treatment Center	3%
Domestic Violence Shelter	1%
Other	7%

	Total Families Housed* N=639
Reunification Status of Families:	
% of Families With One or More Children at Risk of Removal	71%
% of Families With One or More Children in Need of Reunification	29%

	Children in Need of Reunification* N=348
Living Arrangements of <u>Children in Need of Reunification</u>:	
Foster Care	61%
Kinship Foster Care	5%
Relative's Home	26%
Non-Relative's Home	2%
Group Home	6%
Other Institutional Settings	8%

* Includes all families on whom we have received a CWA Referral Form as of 12/1/95.

V. SERVICE NEEDS UPON REFERRAL

	Total Families Housed N=557*
% of Families Reported by Case Workers to Need:	
Housing Search Assistance	75%
Family or Adult Counseling/Mental Health Services	42%
Parenting Classes	41%
Money Management/Budgeting	38%
Transportation	37%
Adult Education/Employment Services	35%
Food, Clothing, Other Goods	31%
Child Counseling/Mental Health Services	25%
Child Care	25%
Child Education	23%
Entitlements	22%
Adult Substance Abuse Services	21%
Health Care	19%
Domestic Violence Services	17%

* Includes all families on whom we have received a CWA Referral Form as of 12/1/95. At some sites this data was not reported since case workers did not fill out the services section.

VI. SECTION 8 HOUSING DATA

Time From Issuance of Section 8 Certificate/Voucher to Lease-Up

Sites* N=688	Average # Days to Lease-Up	Range of Days to Lease-Up (Lowest # to Highest #)
All Sites	50 days	(0–200 days)
A	27 days	(7–131 days)
B	40 days	(3–138 days)
C	42 days	(8–147 days)
D	43 days	(7–154 days)
E	56 days	(6–200 days)
F	57 days	(12–180 days)
G	60 days	(8–144 days)
H	64 days	(16–149 days)
I	71 days	(11–180 days)
J	84 days	(9–198 days)

* Only sites with PHA Lease-Up data on 25 or more families are listed individually. Sites submitting HUD 50058 forms are not included in this chart as the HUD form does not include the date the certificate/voucher was issued.

Total Families Housed *
N = 955

Bedroom Sizes of Units Leased-Up

1 Bedroom	2%
2 Bedrooms	42%
3 Bedrooms	45%
4 Bedrooms	10%
5 Bedrooms	1%

Average Bedroom Size = 2.7

*Includes all families on whom we have received a PHA Lease-Up/50058 Form as of 12/1/95.

Appendix K

Expanded Definition of Federal Preferences, Massachusetts

EXECUTIVE
OFFICE OF
COMMUNITIES &
DEVELOPMENT

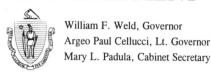

William F. Weld, Governor
Argeo Paul Cellucci, Lt. Governor
Mary L. Padula, Cabinet Secretary

March 3, 1995

Mr. Stan Sigel
Housing Management Specialist
Office of Public Housing
U.S. Department of Housing and Urban Development
Thomas P. O'Neill, Jr. Federal Building
10 Causeway Street
Boston, MA 02222-1092

RE: Family Unification Program -- Request for Approval of Administrative Plan Revision

Dear Mr. Sigel:

In our experience with the Family Unification Program (FUP) to date, we have encountered several cases where we have been unable to assist families because they did not meet the eligibility criteria as narrowly defined in the program regulations. A FUP eligible family is defined in the 1994 NOFA at II(A)(1)(a) as a family that:

     (i)   the public child welfare agency has certified is a family for whom the *lack of adequate housing* is a primary factor in the imminent placement of the family's child, or children, in out-of-home care, or in the delay of discharge of a child, or children, to the family from out-of -home care; and

     (ii)   The HA has determined is eligible for section 8 rental assistance.

     (b)   The *lack of adequate housing* means a situation in which a family:
          (i)   Is living in substandard housing or homeless, as defined in 24 CFR 882.219(f), [now found at 982.212]; or
          (ii)   Is, or will be, involuntarily displaced from a housing unit because of actual or threatened violence against a family member under the circumstances described in 24 CFR 882.219(d)(2) [now found at 982.211(b)(4)].

At issue is the definition of *"adequate housing"*. Frequently an applicant is underhoused; that is, living in a unit that is inadequate for the reunified family size and cannot have their children

100 Cambridge Street
Boston, Massachusetts 02202-0044

returned due to insufficient space. Others may be in doubled-up situations. Where an applicant is doubled-up as a result of domestic violence they are eligible under 982.211(b)(4) -- involuntarily displaced due to domestic violence. If an applicant is doubled-up as a result of having vacated substandard housing meeting the definition at 982.212, they would also be found eligible. However there are applicants in doubled-up situations that do not fall into either of these categories. The doubled-up applicant is not considered a "homeless family" because although they may lack a fixed, regular, and adequate nighttime residence; they do not meet the second part of that definition under parts 982.212 (c)(2)(ii)(A, B, or C).

In these cases, the applicants have complied with their service plan and the Department of Social Services (DSS) is ready to reunite the family, but lack of adequate housing is preventing the reunification. Although housing is the only obstacle to reunification, because the applicant's situation does not meet the definition of "substandard housing" or "homeless family" we are unable to assist them. The federal preference for substandard housing is defined at 982.212 as follows:

    (a)   When a unit is substandard. A unit is substandard if the unit:
        (1)   Is dilapidated;
        (2)   Does not have operable indoor plumbing;
        (3)   Does not have a usable flush toilet inside the unit for the exclusive use of a family;
        (4)   Does not have a usable bathtub or shower inside the unit for the exclusive use of a family;
        (5)   Does not have electricity, or has inadequate or unsafe electrical service;
        (6)   Does not have a safe or adequate source of heat;
        (7)   Should, but does not, have a kitchen; or
        (8)   Has been declared unfit for habitation by an agency or unit of government.

    (b)   Dilapidated unit. A housing unit is dilapidated if:
        (1)   The unit does not provide safe and adequate shelter, and in its present condition endangers the health, safety, or well-being of a family; or
        (2)   The unit has one or more critical defects, or a combination of intermediate defects in sufficient number or extent to require considerable repair or rebuilding. The defects may involve original construction, or they may result from continued neglect or lack of repair or from serious damage to the structure.

    (c)   Homeless family.
        (1)   An applicant that is a homeless family is considered to be living in substandard housing.
        (2)   A "homeless family" includes any person or family that:
            (i)   Lacks a fixed, regular, and adequate nighttime residence; **and also**
            (ii)   Has a primary nighttime residence that is:
                (A)   A supervised publicly or privately operated shelter designed to provide temporary living accommodations (including welfare hotels, congregate shelters, and transitional housing);
                (B)   An institution that provides a temporary residence for persons intended to be institutionalized; or
                (C)   A public or private place not designed for, or ordinarily used as, a regular sleeping accommodation for human beings.

To address this situation EOCD could establish a "local preference". These households could then be assisted but would count against our 10% exception authority. Because there are many competing demands on the use of EOCD's 10% exception authority we are requesting HUD approval to modify the definition of "substandard housing" for the purposes of the Family Unification Program. (The preamble of the Conforming Rule for the Certificate and Voucher Programs, on page 36671 allows a HA to adopt local modifications of the standard preference definitions with HUD field office approval.) We propose to add the following sentence to our FUP Administrative Plan under the definition of substandard housing.

> An applicant will also be considered to be living in substandard housing if the applicant's present unit does not provide adequate space for the family to be reunified according to the Department of Social Services (DSS) occupancy standards.

This expanded definition would allow EOCD to assist applicants who are living in a studio/one bedroom apartment and can not have their children returned due to insufficient space or where the applicant is in a doubled-up situation, e.g., living with a relative and can not be reunited with their children in that situation.

I have discussed these eligibility cases with Paula Callahan of the Department of Social Services, Yvonne Doerre of the Child Welfare League of America and with William Murphy, a Housing Program Specialist on Gerals Benoit's staff who drafted the FUP regulations. There is a general consensus that as written, the eligibility criteria are very narrowly defined and that the intent of the program was not to exclude applicants in the aforementioned situations. HUD approval of this modified definition would allow these families who are in serious need of permanent housing assistance to remain eligible for a federal preference.

Enclosed is a revised version of our FUP administrative plan that includes the alternative definition of substandard housing for your review and approval. The revisions also reflect the statewide expansion of the program as well as the changes as a result of the October 18, 1994 Conforming Rule.

There are several families presently on our FUP waiting lists that will be affected by this decision so we would appreciate your prompt response. If you have any questions or require further information please call me at (617) 727-7130 x.640. Thank you.

Very truly yours,

Jennie L. Rawski
Program Specialist
Bureau of Federal Rental Assistance

cc: Paula Callahan, DSS
        William Murphy, HUD
        Yvonne Doerre, CWLA

MASSACHUSETTS EXECUTIVE OFFICE OF COMMUNITIES AND DEVELOPMENT

FAMILY UNIFICATION PROGRAM
ADMINISTRATIVE PLAN

This revision of The Executive Office of Communities and Development's (EOCD) Family Unification Program (FUP) Administrative Plan addresses the statewide expansion of the program as of January 1, 1995. All references herein are to the regulations currently in effect for the Section 8 Certificate and Voucher programs, as they may be amended. Except as expressly provided herein, all of the provisions of EOCD's Administrative Plan for the Section 8 Certificate and Voucher programs apply to the FUP.

TARGET POPULATION

EOCD, in concert with the Massachusetts Department of Social Services (DSS), has agreed to target the following two populations for FUP consideration:

- battered women and their children who have been displaced because of the battering situation and have not secured permanent, standard, replacement housing; and

- families with children in placement who have substantially complied with all DSS service plan tasks but do not have permanent or adequate housing to which their children can be returned.

CRITERIA FOR PROGRAM ELIGIBILITY

- **Federal Preferences**

The family must demonstrate that they meet at least one of HUD's federal preferences as defined at 24 CFR Section 982.211(b)(4) or 982.212, as amended. Both of these federal preferences are targeted towards households who lack adequate housing.

Involuntarily Displaced Due to Domestic Violence
Section 982.211(b)(4)   [formerly 882.219(d)(2)]

The applicant has vacated a housing unit because of domestic violence; or the applicant lives in a housing unit with a person who engages in domestic violence.

"Domestic violence" means actual or threatened physical violence directed against one or more members of the applicant family by a spouse or other member of the applicant's household.

For an applicant to qualify under this category the actual or threatened violence must have occurred recently or be of a continuing nature and the applicant must certify that the person who engaged in such violence will not reside with the applicant family unless the HA has given advance written approval.

Substandard Housing   *Section 982.212 [formerly 882.219 (f)]*

According to 24 CFR 982.212 (a) and (b) an applicant is living in substandard housing if the unit:
* is dilapidated;
* does not have operable indoor plumbing;
* does not have a usable flush toilet inside the unit for the exclusive use of the family;
* does not have a usable shower or bathtub inside the unit for the exclusive use of the family;
* does not have electricity or has inadequate or unsafe electrical service;
* does not have a safe or adequate source of heat;
* should, but does not have a kitchen; or
* has been declared unfit for habitation by an agency or unit of government

For purposes of meeting substandard criteria, "dilapidated" means the unit does not provide safe and adequate shelter, and in its present condition endangers the health, safety or well-being of a family, or the unit has one or more critical defects, or a combination of intermediate defects in sufficient number or extent to require considerable repair or rebuilding. The defects may involve original construction, or they may result from continued neglect or lack of repair, or from serious damage to the structure.

An applicant that is a homeless family is considered to be living in substandard housing. A "homeless family" includes any person or family that:

- Lacks a fixed, regular, and adequate nighttime residence; **and also**
- Has a primary nighttime residence that is:
  - A supervised publicly or privately operated shelter designed to provide temporary living accommodations (including welfare hotels, congregate shelters, and transitional housing);
  - An institution that provides a temporary residence for persons intended to be institutionalized; or
  - A public or private place not designed for, or ordinarily used as, a regular sleeping accommodation for human beings.

An applicant will also be considered to be living in substandard housing if the applicant's present unit does not provide adequate space for the family to be reunified according to the Department of Social Services (DSS) occupancy standards.

- **Residency Preference**

A regional residency preference for selection will be applied to all FUP applicants. The residency preference areas are the jurisdictions of EOCD's regional administering agencies This residency preference does not preclude FUP applicants from applying at any of EOCD's regional administering agencies.

If an applicant family is living in a shelter or other temporary residence, the location of their last permanent residence shall be used for the purpose of establishing a residency preference.

- **Other Eligibility Criteria**

Applicants must have an open DSS case at the time of application, at the time of selection, and at the time a subsidy is issued.

The family must be otherwise Section 8 eligible.

EOCD Section 8 FUP Administrative Plan

OUTREACH

Each EOCD regional administering agency must satisfy the FUP requirement that current applicants on their conventional Section 8 waiting list be given first opportunity to indicate an interest in the FUP program. This will be accomplished by placing a public notice in a newspaper(s) of general regional circulation that will reach both majority and minority populations, requesting that any household currently on the conventional regional agency's Section 8 waiting list who believes that they may be eligible for the FUP, notify the regional administering agency and request a FUP application.

The public notice must conform to HUD requirements for public advertising and must also include the following statements:

- only applicants with an open DSS case plan at the time they apply for the FUP will be considered eligible; and,

- a residency preference for selection will be given to eligible applicants.

A list of the regional administering agency's communities must be included in the ad.

For administrative convenience, the housing agency may limit the number of applications taken in response to any FUP outreach.

MAINTAINING A FUP WAITING LIST

In accordance with the October 18, 1994, conforming rule on admissions each of EOCD's regional administering agencies will maintain a separate FUP waiting list and issue any available subsidies without regard to bedroom size.

<u>For agencies with an open Section 8 conventional waiting list</u>

EOCD's standard Section 8 application, in use as of 10/94, allows applicants to self-identify as being eligible for the FUP. EOCD and DSS have prepared a FUP fact sheet that should be provided to all Section 8 applicants at the same time they receive the Section 8 application. If an applicant believes that they are eligible for the FUP they should request and submit the FUP application at that time. The burden is on the applicant to request the FUP application.

If a FUP application is submitted, they will be placed on both the FUP list and the conventional Section 8 waiting list. Any new FUP applicant will be placed at the bottom of the regional administering agency's FUP waiting list based on the date and time their FUP application is submitted. If found ineligible for the FUP, they will retain their place on the conventional Section 8 waiting list.

For agencies with a closed Section 8 conventional waiting list

If the regional administering agency has a closed conventional Section 8 waiting list and has not been able to generate enough interest from eligible applicants on their current waiting list, the regional agency is permitted to open a waiting list for Family Unification eligible families only. In this instance, HUD requires that the agency advertise the opening of its FUP waiting list before accepting new applicants.

If these applicants are later found ineligible for the FUP they will be dropped from the FUP list. These applicants are not placed on the conventional Section 8 waiting list because it was closed at the time they applied for the FUP.

MANAGING REFERRALS

DSS Area Office Referrals to the FUP

DSS Area Offices can make referrals to any open FUP waiting list by submitting a referral form to the regional administering agency. At the housing agency the applicant will fill out a FUP application and be placed on the FUP waiting list. The regional administering agency will perform the standard Section 8 eligibility check involving income verification, preference status in conformance with Section 982.211(b)(4) and 982.212, household composition, and where applicable, CORI status. If the applicant is found to be Section 8 eligible the application is forwarded to the Central/Regional Office screening staff for review to ensure eligibility. The Central/Regional Office screening staff will inform both the regional administering agency and the area office of the applicant's eligibility or ineligibility in writing.

<u>Housing Agency Referrals to DSS</u>

FUP applicants must complete a FUP application in which they self-certify that they have an open DSS case on the date on which they applied for the FUP. The applicant must also identify the DSS Area office that manages their case, and when possible, indicate the name and phone number of their DSS case worker.

If the applicant appears to be eligible for the FUP, EOCD's regional administering agency will refer the applicant to the DSS Central/Regional Office screening staff for verification of status as an open DSS case in one of the two target categories. DSS Central/Regional office staff will contact the assigned case worker and inform him/her of the referral to the FUP and the program eligibility requirements. If the assigned case worker can verify eligibility and supports the FUP referral, he/she will forward to Central/Regional Office a brief information sheet documenting eligibility.

If the applicant receives the DSS FUP certification, the applicant returns to the regional administering agency for the standard Section 8 eligibility check, involving income verification, preference status in conformance with Section 982.211(b)(4) and 982.212, household composition, and where applicable, CORI status.

At this point, if the applicant is found to be eligible the subsidy is issued, and all normal Section 8 procedures take place, beginning with a briefing session. DSS staff are welcome to attend all Section 8 related functions with their clients and are encouraged to help them locate suitable and safe housing.

In the event that referrals from EOCD's regional administering agency's exceed the capacity of the Central/Regional office screening staff to be processed on a timely basis, the regional housing agencies may be directed to refer directly to the DSS Area offices after a suitable protocol is established.

PARTICIPANT SELECTION

Selection for the FUP will be done based on the date and time of the FUP application submission. FUP subsidies will be issued based on the date and time of the DSS Central/Regional Office eligibility approval. There may be instances where because of unreasonable delays in the application process on either the part of the applicant or DSS, the regional administering agency may choose to issue to a subsequent referral for the (first) available subsidy.

EOCD Section 8 FUP Administrative Plan (3/95)

6

In such cases, the regional administering agency will document clearly in the applicant file why such a decision was made. The applicant who is skipped will be issued the next available FUP subsidy provided they submit the required documentation.

APPEALS

EOCD's regional administering agencies are responsible for defending their eligibility decisions, pertaining to the family's eligibility for Section 8 rental assistance. Section 8 informal hearing procedures will be utilized and shall be the same as currently in effect for Section 8 participants, as set forth in the Administrative Plan for Certificates and Vouchers.

The DSS is responsible for defending its family eligibility determinations and a similar informal hearing procedure will be utilized.

ON-GOING CONSIDERATIONS

All FUP subsidies will be issued to other FUP eligible applicants upon turnover.

Regional administering agencies will participate in all required evaluations, and will be prepared to maintain additional data on these clients, as required by HUD and/or DSS.

After the subsidy is issued, DSS will inform the housing agency of any changes in the family's situation or composition, such as the permanent removal of the children from the household.

Appendix L

Regional HUD's Instruction on the Temporary Absence of a Child

This is a transcription of an original signed letter from HUD regional office.

U.S. Department of Housing and Urban Development
Seattle Office, Region X
Arcade Plaza Building
1321 Second Avenue
Seattle, Washington 98101-2054

PHA CIRCULAR	February 28, 1992

ATTENTION: ALL PUBLIC HOUSING AGENCIES	**No 92-8**
SUBJECT: Effect of Foster Care Children in Determining Family Composition and Size: Section 574 of the Cranston-Gonzalez National Affordable Housing Act	**Applies to:** LIPH Section 8

It has recently come to our attention that some PHAs may not be aware of the provisions of Section 574 of the Cranston-Gonzalez National Affordable Housing Act regarding the effect of children placed in foster care when determining family composition and family size. The purpose of the Circular is to highlight this provision of the Act and to ensure that PHAs in the State of Washington are administering assisted programs in compliance with Section 574.

Section 574 of the Cranston-Gonzalez National Affordable Housing Act states:

> The temporary absence of a child from the home due to placement in foster care shall not be considered in considering family composition and family size.

In the Public Housing and the Section 8 programs, PHAs routinely make determinations regarding the bedroom size of the unit, the size of the Certificate or the size of the Voucher, for which a family qualifies. These determinations are based on "Occupancy Standards" established by a PHA. Such standards outline a minimum and maximum number of family members necessary to qualify for a given bedroom size.

Essentially, Section 574 directs PHAs to disregard the temporary absence of a child from the home due to placement of the child in foster care, when making determinations on family size, family composition, and the bedroom size of the unit, Certificate, or Voucher for which the family qualified. When making such determinations for a given family, based on the PHA's Occupancy Standards, the PHA should include the child (or children) *temporarily* absent in foster care as family member(s).

In the Public Housing program, HUD issued a revision to Handbook 7465.1, *The Public Housing Occupancy Handbook: Admissions,* which clarified the nation on February 12,1991. The revisions amended Paragraph 5-1.a(6) of the Handbook, which now reads:

> For the purpose of determining unit size, PHAs are required to include, as members of the household, all children anticipated to reside in a dwelling unit.

The PHA should also include children who are temporarily absent from the home due to placement in foster care when considering family composition and family size.

To our knowledge, similar revisions have not yet been made to HUD Handbook 7420.7, *The Section 8 Existing Administrative Handbook*.

In summary, when making determinations regarding **family size and composition,** and **appropriate unit size,** for families in the Public Housing program, or in the Section 8 programs, please ensure that the provisions of Section 574 are followed. Children who are **temporarily** absent from the family due to placement in foster care should be counted as members of the household.

Sincerely,

Harold E. Saether
Director, Office of Public Housing

About the Authors

Yvonne A. Doerre has coordinated the Family Unification Program (FUP) at CWLA since 1994. She began her work in housing and child welfare as an intern with the Missouri Department of Social Services, where she served as case manager for families participating in FUP. At CWLA she conducted a national survey that provided the first wide-scale outcome data for the program. She leads national and regional training conferences and provides technical assistance to agencies across the country as they implement programs that coordinate housing, child welfare, and social services for children and families. Doerre is a graduate of Indiana University and the George Warren School of Social Work at Washington University, St. Louis, Missouri.

Lisa Mihaly has been an advocate for low-income children and families for more than 10 years, focusing on child poverty, housing, homelessness, child welfare, child abuse, and domestic violence. At the Children's Defense Fund in Washington, D.C., she was instrumental in the establishment of the Family Unification Program. As an independent consultant, she has provided policy analysis and technical assistance to nonprofit organizations and local government agencies. She now works for the San Francisco Starting Points Initiative, a new effort to plan and implement improved services for children under five. She is a graduate of Harvard University.